MAKING THE MOST OF DIGITAL COLLECTIONS THROUGH TRAINING AND OUTREACH

**Recent Title in Libraries Unlimited's
Innovative Librarian's Guide Series**

Digitizing Audiovisual and Nonprint Materials:
The Innovative Librarian's Guide
Scott Piepenburg

MAKING THE MOST OF DIGITAL COLLECTIONS THROUGH TRAINING AND OUTREACH

The Innovative Librarian's Guide

Nicholas Tanzi

INNOVATIVE LIBRARIAN'S GUIDE

LIBRARIES UNLIMITED™

An Imprint of ABC-CLIO, LLC

Santa Barbara, California • Denver, Colorado

Library of Congress Cataloging-in-Publication Data

Names: Tanzi, Nicholas, author.
Title: Making the most of digital collections through training and outreach : the innovative librarian's guide / Nicholas Tanzi.
Description: Santa Barbara, CA : Libraries Unlimited, [2016] | Series: Innovative librarian's guide | Includes bibliographical references and index.
Identifiers: LCCN 2015031398| ISBN 9781440840722 (paperback) | ISBN 9781440840739 (ebook)
Subjects: LCSH: Libraries—Special collections—Electronic information resources. | BISAC: LANGUAGE ARTS & DISCIPLINES / Library & Information Science / Collection Development. | LANGUAGE ARTS & DISCIPLINES / Library & Information Science / Cataloging & Classification.
Classification: LCC Z692.C65 T36 2016 | DDC 025.2/84—dc23
LC record available at http://lccn.loc.gov/2015031398

ISBN: 978-1-4408-4072-2
EISBN: 978-1-4408-4073-9

20 19 18 17 16   1 2 3 4 5

This book is also available on the World Wide Web as an eBook.
Visit www.abc-clio.com for details.

Libraries Unlimited
An Imprint of ABC-CLIO, LLC

ABC-CLIO, LLC
130 Cremona Drive, P.O. Box 1911
Santa Barbara, California 93116-1911

This book is printed on acid-free paper ∞

Manufactured in the United States of America

Contents

Acknowledgments

I wish to express my gratitude to:

My friends and family for their encouragement.

My coworkers at the community library for their hard work and dedication to public service, which allows our organization to flourish.

Thank you to the following individuals without whose contributions and support this book would not have been written:

My wife, Kristine, for her love (always) and support during the writing process. Patience is a virtue and she showed an abundance of it while I delayed painting the baby's room.

Sara Roye, graphic artist extraordinaire. Her skill in design is matched only by her generosity.

Dan Costa for checking my math and supplying advice and sarcasm in equal measure.

Lise Dyckman for guiding me along the winding road that leads from a concept to a published book.

Introduction

The Challenges Facing a Library's Digital Collection

In just a few short years, library collections have gone increasingly digital. According to *Library Journal*, in 2014, 95 percent of public libraries now offer eBooks to their patrons (Factually 2014). Far from being an amenity, eBooks have become an expectation. In addition to eBooks, libraries are adding to their collection streaming movies and music, audiobooks and eMagazines. We've come a long way! However, as is often the case with change, there have been challenges.

As Head of the Digital Services Department at the Mastics-Moriches-Shirley Community Library (MMSCL), a great deal of my responsibilities involves the library's digital collection. I am responsible for overseeing the acquisition of digital books, audiobooks, movies, music, and magazines. I likewise manage staff and patron technology training, including the use of the library's digital collection.

MMSCL is a large library serving 60,000 patrons across four towns, plus contract patrons from three additional towns, who have the option to renew their cards with us annually. We are part of a loose consortium of libraries in Suffolk County, New York, who pool some resources together in the form of consolidated orders, but exercise a tremendous amount of autonomy. We serve a diverse community with large disparity in income. Many of our patrons rely on public transportation. While these complexities present their own unique set of challenges, our patrons' and staff members' experiences in trying to access eContent are very similar to what's happening in public libraries all over the country. Based on what we've seen, I have identified the following barriers to a successful digital collection.

LACK OF AWARENESS

While the majority of libraries are offering eBook services, it is also true that the majority of our patrons are unaware of them! According to the American Library Association, 60 percent of library patrons don't know their library lends eBooks (Forbes 2014). A library's digital collection is doomed to failure if the majority of our stakeholders don't know it exists. If our patrons don't know about our eBook collection, chances are they're not looking for emerging library services such as streaming music and video. Digital collections are ideal for the patron who doesn't walk through your door on a regular basis—but how do you reach them?

BAD PRIOR EXPERIENCE

Perhaps more detrimental to the success of a library's digital collection is not the patron who is unaware of our service, but the patron who tried and was dissatisfied with it. In the early days of library eBook services, the user interface was often poorly constructed, particularly when compared with commercial models (NOOK store, Amazon). Digital Rights Management (DRM), intended to protect copyright, was cumbersome and could present a barrier to downloading an eBook. Additionally, many devices were not compatible with some eBook services. Overdrive, for example, experienced a period during which their collection was incompatible with the Amazon Kindle. The Kindle is a dominant force in eReading, and libraries were left turning away these patrons. While some have undoubtedly discovered they can now borrow eBooks from their library, who's to say how many are still under the impression that they cannot? Clearly, we must create a better user experience. This improved model must then be communicated to our patrons.

LACK OF FAMILIARITY

Imagine yourself at the car dealership. The salesman is trying to get you to buy the latest model sports car, but is unable to answer your questions. Gas mileage? Not sure. What type of engine? Let me talk to one of the other salespeople. Upon further investigation, it's clear he's never even driven before! In this scenario, it's pretty unlikely that you're buying a car from that dealership. Without a firm grasp of your library's digital collection, it is likely that the staff will have comparable interactions with the public. To many, the idea of borrowing digital materials from their library is a new one, and they look for the staff to instill confidence in them, and not further confuse them.

Unfortunately, staff training is a journey, not a destination. Even if you could snap your fingers and magically train all your library's staff in a service's use, how long would that dream scenario last? Services are subject to change over time. Your institution will experience turnover and new staff will need to be trained. Staff members who don't continue using the service will forget their training. Your library will undoubtedly add new digital collections, which will require instructing them on its use.

HESITANCY BY THE PUBLIC TO TRY SOMETHING NEW

To a lot of people, change is uncomfortable. Many of your patrons are used to borrowing traditional print and analog media from their library. The idea of borrowing digital media is a new one. As a precursor to borrowing library digital media, your patrons will likely need an e-mail address. While most do have one, not all will. A more substantial requirement is that they must have a computer, laptop, smartphone, eReader, or tablet. Those that do not may be hesitant to go out and purchase one as a precursor to using services they are unfamiliar with.

To be clear, we should always seek to tailor library services to our patrons and not attempt to change patron behavior to fit them. That being said, we have a responsibility to provide community access to materials that are increasingly digital. While the majority of books are available in print format, we are seeing an increase in "digital only" publications, particularly those spearheaded by Amazon. The patron who isn't reading digitally loses access to that title. When reserving print materials for patrons, you will find that while many people have a favored format (hardcover, paperback, large print, etc.) there are some who will take whatever they can get the quickest. A patron who denies himself the digital copy loses what may be the quickest path to his desired material. If there are ways to take the fear of the unknown out of the equation, shouldn't we?

LOW DIGITAL LITERACY AMONG SOME PATRONS

Just because a person owns a tablet, eReader, laptop, smartphone, or other digital device, it is in no way an indication that he is comfortable using it. A patron might have qualified for a free upgrade to an Android smartphone, but she is lost now that she has it. While their local carrier may take some time to show them the basics of their phone, I can assure you they will not be going over how to consume library digital media! Gadgets are a popular gift, particularly around the holidays. Someone may have bought their friend or loved one a device that has sat unused since it didn't come with a personalized lesson! When that lesson was given, it often involved a particular function or application: "here's how you play solitaire" or "this is how to FaceTime."

During my time running digital services at MMSCL, I have engaged in a multifaceted approach to ensure the success of our collection. While these challenges I have outlined are many, it is also true that necessity is the mother of invention. This book seeks to help you, the reader, overcome these obstacles through the following:

STAFF TRAINING

This book will describe a *device-centric*, rather than service-oriented, approach to staff training. I will explain exactly what this approach is, how it works, and its benefits. I will go over the process of developing a curriculum to serve your library and its staff members. I'll list the equipment you'll need to conduct training in a way that can be scaled to the size of your library. With the understanding that training can require a tremendous amount of staff time, I'll outline ways of utilizing a user-directed approach. This approach can greatly reduce the need for instructors and can help minimize disruption to reference desk coverage. Finally, once you have the necessary curriculum and equipment, I will describe how you can institutionalize the training so that staff proficiencies are not lost over time.

PATRON INSTRUCTION

A patron who does not understand how her iPad works will never borrow eBooks, stream movies and music, or use any other portion of your library's digital collection. A patron who has a level of comfort with her device, but finds the library's eContent confusing to use, is likely to ignore it and perhaps turn to commercial models. In order to maximize patron use of your collection, you must instruct patrons in the basic use of their computers and mobile devices *and* offer instruction on the use of library digital services. As people learn differently, there is no one-size-fits-all approach.

Acknowledging this fact, I will describe a variety of approaches from one-on-one to group instruction. In the case of one-on-one instruction, I'll describe how you can set up an appointment-based tech help service for your patrons. For group instruction of patrons, you'll be provided with a curriculum in addition to information on setup and execution of classes.

PROMOTION

The best way to combat a lack of awareness of the library's digital collection is, of course, to promote it. In the case of a library's digital collection, however, this can be tricky. Libraries have become very good at in-house advertising, with a multitude of posters, flyers, book displays, and digital signage. How does one make a book display for an eBook? How effective can a poster or flyer be if the ultimate destination is web based? This book will provide simple, low-cost setups for interactive displays showcasing your library's eContent. With the correct elements, print signage can be an effective way of promoting your digital services.

In addition to in-house advertising, we'll talk about social media marketing and web-based advertising, providing a list of best practices. I'll cover some in-the-box promotions you can run alongside summer or winter reading clubs or on their own. Finally, this book will show you how you can establish a device lending program to allow patrons to "try before they buy," as a way of selling your digital collection to them before they make a financial commitment.

OUTREACH

Very much a part of promotion, outreach has the potential to greatly expand the use of your digital collection. A portion of your patrons have difficulty in making it to the library, whether it is because of distance, lack of transportation, or other factors. While your digital collection doesn't require these patrons to enter your building, they may be unaware of its existence or unable to get started. Getting out to these underserved patrons where they are creates library users where previously there were none. So how do you bring a digital branch with you?

I'll cover how to create a mobile presence you can take with you to an array of venues, from schools, supermarkets, public buildings to even the beach! As the venues may vary, so too will the setups. This book will describe how you can use a mix of devices and sample accounts to succeed in areas with poor or even no Wi-Fi signal.

SAVING MONEY

Let's face it—technology can be expensive. Not only is it expensive, but it is also apt to change, quickly becoming outmoded and eventually obsolete. Some of the training and promotional techniques within this book do call for you to purchase various devices. While you may be hesitant to spend on mobile devices, you must view these outlays as a cost saver! While this may at first seem counterintuitive, think about it. Your library is dedicating ever larger portions of its operating budget to digital media. If you can increase the circulation of your collection, the cost per circulation will decrease, saving you money.

Happily, there are other ways to stretch a technology budget. We'll look at ways of resource sharing to reduce the burden on your individual organization. We'll discuss potential sources of free content, devices, and help from volunteers. When you do purchase mobile devices, this book will cover how you can repurpose them to maximize their use. A new use for a device can often mean an extended life. We'll look at the development of a replacement schedule for your equipment. Such a schedule will allow you to anticipate future expenditures and responsibly manage your costs. With all these cost-saving features in hand, you will ensure that purchases can be justified as necessary and beneficial to the library's operation. We'll examine ways to frame the positive effect individual services, equipment, and training can have on your digital collection. This information can then be used to help convince a hesitant library administration of its necessity if resistance exists.

Where challenges exist, so too does opportunity. In the following chapters, we'll examine solutions. This book will line up the numerous challenges facing a library's digital collection and one by one remove them. With the understanding that libraries differ in the community they serve, their budget, locale, and any other number of factors, the techniques here are adaptable. Techniques can be taken à la carte. They can be scaled to the size of your institution. No one knows the community you serve better than you, and it is my intent that you wed that knowledge with the information that is to follow.

Chapter 1

Staff Training

When you are preparing to train staff, the first thing you must determine is exactly who needs to know what. In the case of your library's digital collection, it is not necessary that all staff members know everything, but all must know something. At the same time, it makes no sense to overtrain staff in a service that they are unlikely to use in their job at the library. Balance is key. The training you invest in each individual must be commensurate with the likelihood it will be needed. This will result in layers of training.

So what is that "something" that everyone needs to know? It's awareness of the digital collection. If we were talking about the library's physical collection, you would find it wholly unacceptable if a staff member didn't know you lent books! Despite this, it is not uncommon to have certain members of your organization unaware of eBooks, streaming music, or other parts of the digital collection simply because they don't interact with it in their day-to-day responsibilities. Unlike the physical collection, it's not staring them in the face. Unless you have taken the time to introduce and orient staff to your collection, you cannot expect them to know about it.

LAYER ONE: BUILDING AWARENESS OF
THE DIGITAL COLLECTION

Assume for a moment that your library has just added a new eBook service. Your first priority must be to ensure all staff members know the basics of it. For your purposes, the basics are simply the same information a patron would need to know to use the service.

- What is it?
- Where can I find it?
- How does it work?
- Why should I use it?

A good practice when adding a new service is to use your staff as a test run. Generally, when you have a new addition to your library, there is a gap between that happening and your public learning about it through your newsletter, social media, word of mouth, and so forth. Since this level of training only requires that your staff members know what a patron needs to know, you can use them as a stand-in for your public at large. The following are some simple techniques for doing a soft launch.

Schedule an Open House

An open house is simply a series of drop-in opportunities for staff to learn about your new (in this case eBook) service. With the understanding that your goal is to expose all staff to the service, communication is key. Depending on how you disseminate information at your library, this could be e-mails, message board, intranet, or other message communicated by the heads of each department. You'll likely need to offer an evening and weekend session to ensure that part-time staff members are included. These open-house events should be roughly 20 minutes long, allowing you to schedule three per hour, centered around swing shifts, if the size of your library dictates. This will allow you to expose staff to a service without disrupting the operation of the various departments.

Setup

Like any great sales pitch, visuals are important. When you're advertising this service to the public, you'll likely have posters and flyers run off. Have these done in advance and placed in the room where you're conducting orientation. This should be the first thing your staff sees, as it builds an expectation of the service you're talking about prior to them seeing the actual service demonstrated. If you find the two are very different, then perhaps you need to redesign your print materials! In a subsequent chapter, I will give some specific design tips regarding print advertisements.

If possible, you should have several tablets available so staff members have the opportunity to get "hands on" in the case that they don't have their own. Not all services work on all devices, so be sure that you are in possession of those compatible with what you're showing! Generally speaking, this will involve an iPad and an Android tablet as they are versatile enough to work with most eBook, music, and video services.

Remembering that time is of the essence, you'll want to have "dummy" accounts on these devices so your staff can dive right into the experience. These dummy accounts will consist of e-mail addresses that multiple staff can all access. Additionally, you will generate some mock patron accounts in your integrated library system (ILS). When making your mock patrons, consider making a range of patron types, including juvenile and young adult (YA) (if applicable). Some digital collections can be age restricted and you'll want to ensure these safeguards are operating correctly. Additionally, this can be a selling point to your audience.

Continuing with our setup, a laptop with a projector will allow you to show staff the eMedia site, which would be versatile enough to accommodate small or large groups, plus those with visual impairments. If budget, audience size, or some other factor prevents you from having several tablets available for staff, you can simply provide your presenter with one and connect it to the projector to mirror the screen. This will require a VGA adapter, which is relatively inexpensive.

Presenting

Remember our questions! Starting with the "what is it?" you'll hand flyers to staff as they enter the room. Give them a few moments to look them over before starting with your presentation via the laptop/projector. Don't just tell them what it's called—tell them what it is! "Overdrive" doesn't mean eBooks to anyone not already using it. So while the proprietary name of a service is helpful in differentiating it from other similar services, it doesn't tell anyone what it is. You can also define the relationship. Using the Overdrive example, explain their role as an aggregator. They are not a publisher; rather, they provide a platform for patrons to check out eBooks and other digital materials in a variety of formats.

Moving on to the "where can I find it?" you'll want to go over how to locate the site on your web page. Don't simply type in a direct URL unless that is how you intend your patrons to find it. In the case that you have not yet gone live with it on your website, you'll have to guide staff to where it will ultimately be, up to and including a mock-up of that portion of your web page. This can also be an unpublished or internal version of the web page. In total, this should proceed as follows:

- First we go to our website, MySampleLibrary.com.
- Then we go to "Our Collection."
- Click on "eBooks."
- Finally, click on "the service we're talking about."

Once on the eMedia site, we can address the "how does it work?" question. It is easy to get bogged down in minutiae—remember this is an overview. Is there a sign-up process? Show them. Instruct your audience on how to navigate the collection. How do you locate materials? Is there a browse function, simple and advanced searches? How do you check out/download materials? Answering these few questions is a solid foundation.

In the process of demonstrating the "how does it work?" you should be communicating the "why should I use it." This requires some knowledge of the collection. What are its strengths? Does it have a great selection of kids' books? An expansive collection of horror films? Knowing these details can help you to sell it better. Outside of the collection itself, what about the service? Is it a selling point? Is it convenient? How much could a person save rather than use a commercial model? You want to get staff excited about it.

If you stay on point, this orientation can be completed in under twenty minutes. This leaves you with a bit of time to allow staff to try the services on the tablets with dummy accounts, if you've made them available. Some staff will want to try the service on their personal devices they've brought with them. Let those that are comfortable in trying out the service do so while you answer outstanding audience questions.

Following the Open House

When these sessions end, you will likely find yourself with some homework. While you took time to learn the service prior to showing it to staff, there will be questions you didn't know the answer to. When this happens, be honest. "I don't know, but I'll find out" is far better than coming up with a plausible but incorrect answer. Given that staff will repeat this falsehood, it can quickly add to a confusion that is spread to your patrons. Instead, do your research, locate the correct information, and pass it on to staff. In some cases, you'll be able to make the corrections in between open houses.

When staff saw your flyers and handouts, what was their reaction? Did they feel like it accurately depicted the service? Did they find it confusing, or was key information hard to find or omitted? When your print materials were created, the text was either written or relayed by a person who already had some level of familiarity with the service. While this is of course necessary, it can lead to the author reading it differently from the intended audience. At the end of your last open house, make all necessary corrections to your print materials. A corrected copy of the flyer should make its way to each staff member, as not everyone may have attended the open house.

Next, consider the gadgets in your open house. Either you provided staff with some devices and/or they brought their own personal ones. With the prevalence of smartphones, a good portion of your staff has the opportunity to get hands-on with the service even if they don't own a computer, tablet, or other device. While you've tested what you could in advance, this is the most use the service has seen by your institution at this early time. Looking at the staff-owned devices, the likelihood is that you have broadened the model, brand, and operating systems you've already tested.

Over the next few days, ask for and document staff feedback. How different is the experience across operating systems? While individual digital collections may be said to be compatible with Android, iOS, and other operating systems, understand that there are multiple versions of each. Android, in particular, is licensed to many different manufacturers, leading to a broad range of versions. This means that the term up to date is a relative one. A "brand-new" Android tablet might run an older version of the Android operating system. Generally, you can locate the operating system in the "settings" of most devices, often under "about." When staff indicate problems, take note of the device, operating system, and the result (What was the solution? Was there a solution?). The information you gather here will be added to the more formalized training I'll outline shortly.

At the end of this process, you have instilled a basic awareness of the service in all staff members. Unfortunately, unless staff is using the service either personally or in their day-to-day work, familiarity will fade. New staff may also be unaware of this portion of your collection. As a result, you must institutionalize the open house. This can be fairly simple.

Create a staff proficiency chart: A staff proficiency chart begins with a staff roster, arranged by department and title. Also included is the date of last orientation.

Since all staff members are expected to have this level of training (awareness), this particular chart should include all employees. As your library adds new staff, add them to the roster. If at any point the number of untrained staff members necessitates it, hold another open house. Barring this, plan on engaging in an open house for each digital service you offer once annually. Digital collections are never static, and over time the content, compatible devices, lending rules, and features may all change. Take the most current flyers advertising your digital collections and have them added to the new hire information you give to staff. Staff should read, initial, and return these materials to their supervisor so that they can have some level of familiarity with your services prior to your next open house.

LAYER TWO: FORMALIZED TRAINING OF FRONTLINE STAFF

Thus far, we've covered how to instill a basic level of awareness of your digital collection in all staff members. This level of training will allow your staff to field the simplest of questions. For some patrons, being told what you have, where to find it, and how it works is enough. They'll take this information and effectively use your services. For many, however, they will need a greater level of assistance, and you will need to offer more involved training to your staff to match. I will next describe a device-centric approach that has proven very effective in my organization.

The Device-Centric Approach

At the Mastics-Moriches-Shirley Community Library, we offer eBook, eMagazines, streaming/downloadable music, and two streaming movie services. When I first began training frontline staff on the use of the library's digital collection, I spent an incredible amount of time on the nuances of each of these services. At the outset of library eBook lending, the help offered by many services was poor and incomplete. Some were not yet widely adopted, meaning there was little referral information available. In that deficit, I had staff memorizing the process.

No sooner had I completed a training cycle than a service changed. Often, these changes were for the better, such as an improvement in the look of the website or additional supported formats. Even improvements, however, left some confused and needing additional training. It was clear I needed to come up with a better way for lasting staff instruction. It was out of this need that I employed the device-centric approach to training.

The device-centric approach focuses on the most common devices library patrons will use with a given library digital collection. It is intended for public service staff who would be required to assist a patron in the basic setup and use of a given digital service. Therefore, if your library considers this to be a librarian job, you would limit your training to the librarians. If a collection is not intended for minors, you would likely not instruct your children's staff on the more involved training aspects. With this in mind, let's examine how to execute this method of training.

Building a Curriculum

Consider the service you're training staff on. What devices are compatible with it? If we take an eBook service such as Overdrive, there's a very long list. Among the many supported devices are the iPad, iPod Touch, iPhone, Samsung Galaxy Tab, Nexus 7, Verizon Ellipsis, Kindle Fire, Kindle eReader, Windows Surface Pro Tablets, the NOOK—literally dozens of devices. What we must first do is simplify this list and determine what devices we will need to purchase for staff training.

One of the first ways to do this is by focusing on the operating systems. The iPad, iPhone, and iPod Touch all run on the iOS system. As such, you need not focus on each individually. In this instance, an iPad as a training device would make for a smart purchase. The iPhone and iPod touch are simply too small to serve the purpose, not to mention the phone would be prohibitively expensive (you would need to either purchase a data plan or pay a premium for one without a contract). Outside of iOS, the other major mobile operating system is Android. An enormous number of tablets and smartphones are powered by Android. The Nexus 7 and Samsung Galaxy Tab are inexpensive but powerful Android tablet options. Between Android and iOS, you have accounted for 97.9 percent of the tablet market (Time 2014) and 96 percent of the smartphone market (9to5Mac 2014).

With the iPad and Android tablet, you are off to a good start. You should next consider the Kindle Fire. The Kindle Fire is an extremely popular tablet and you may find many of your patrons own one. The Kindle Fire is actually an Android tablet with an Amazon "skin" or modification which changes the look of the operating system. This difference in appearance is substantial enough to require it to be taught separately from Android.

The remaining mobile operating systems you may encounter are Windows and Blackberry. While a dominant force in personal computers, the Windows mobile operating system has been slow to be adopted. The number of patrons you are likely to encounter utilizing your digital collection using a Windows tablet will be substantially lower than iOS and Android (IDC 2015). Still, every community is different. Unless you notice your patrons commonly using Windows mobile devices, it may not be worth the investment in time to train the frontline staff on it. Looking at Blackberry, this operating system is nearly obsolete and can be ignored.

For most digital media services, this would be enough. In the case of eBooks, however, you must of course consider the eReader. Happily, there is a fairly consistent experience among these devices, requiring that you focus on a current-generation Kindle black-and-white eReader and a non-Kindle eReader, such as a NOOK or Kobo. Between these two devices, you will be able to recreate most patron experiences using a library eBook service.

So we've sorted through a broad range of devices and limited to the ones compatible with the service we're training on. This leaves us with an Android tablet, iPad, Kindle Fire, Kindle eReader, and the NOOK (and perhaps a Windows 8 tablet). In the case of the tablets, you should check to make sure they are capable of running the most current version of their respective operating system. With your Kindle and NOOK, simply find a current-generation model.

We have our devices. We have chosen the (eBook) service we're training on. We have defined the staff we intend to train: frontline staff required to assist patrons in setting up the service. What we need now is a curriculum.

Developing a Curriculum

One of the keys to device-centric training is first building mobile competency. Simply put, staff must be comfortable with the basic use of the devices we just identified. This comfort will prove helpful when it is later applied to your digital services. For tablets, the basics are the following:

The Basic Anatomy of the Device The focus here is the hardware. Where is the power button located? Where are the volume control and speakers? Is there a camera? Is there a home button, menu, or other hardware controls?

Starting Up How do you power on/power off? How do you lock and unlock the screen? How do you restart or, in the case of a frozen device, hard reset?

Touch Gestures Explain the various touch gestures used to operate a tablet. Generally speaking, these are swipe, tap, pinch, stretch, touch and hold, and turn.

Basic Settings You can easily get overwhelmed by the sheer number of options. Focus on the most important features. At the top of the list is how to locate and connect to Wi-Fi. Also consider the screen and security settings. How do you change the time it takes for the screen to lock? How do you lock/unlock the screen orientation?

Using the Tablet's Web Browser While there are many mobile web browsers now available, focus on the default one for the device you are training on. Identify the browser icon. How do you search or surf? How do you add bookmarks and favorites? How do you open/close tabs?

Apps Where is the device's app store? How do you navigate it? How do you install as well as remove an app? How are apps organized?

In the case of an eReader, what you cover will vary slightly. You will again touch upon the basic anatomy of the device, how to start up, and basic settings. You will cover a more narrow number of touch gestures that apply. Some eReaders have a very basic web browser that can be shown. eReaders do not have an app store, meaning you can skip this portion of the curriculum.

Covering these items will leave a staff member with a basic understanding of the device. Once this foundation is laid, you must next pair it with the digital collection. Continuing with our sample eBook service, we must now cover its basic use. This would include the following:

How to Create an Account Surely you'll need a library card, but what else? Do you need a separate account for the service, such as a username and password? Does it require that you download an app? Do you need to choose your library from a list?

How to Navigate the Collection How do you find what you're looking for? What types of searches can you perform? Is there a browse option? Is everything always available, or are there a limited number of copies?

How to Checkout Once you've located the item you want, how do you check it out? What is the download process? Do you need to choose between file types? Where does it go once downloaded?

How to "Use" Your Checked Out Item If it's an eBook, how do you turn the page? How is the font size and color changed? How do you add a bookmark? For audio and video collections, how do you play, skip, stop, and pause? Can you make a playlist? If you have a choice between downloading and streaming, how does it work? For video, are there subtitles?

How to Return Once you're done with a digital item, how is it returned? Does it remove itself when it expires? Can you return it early? Expired items, while unusable, may still take up space on a device. While eBook files are very small, video and audio files can really eat into a device's storage.

How to Use Help Nearly all services offer a help section. Where is it located? Is it searchable or do you browse topics? In the event that the help is inadequate or nonexistent, your library should work to have some FAQs and basic troubleshooting in place.

Turning a Curriculum into a Lesson

We now have a curriculum that covers both common devices and how to use your services. Our next step is to create an audiovisual lesson that will be used in a training station. This station will give you the flexibility of both user-directed and staff-assisted training. If this sounds complicated, don't worry—it's not! You'll only need an Internet connection and Microsoft Office (or free word processing software like Google Docs). You can of course use a basic blog format using free or inexpensive options such as Blogger (Blogger 2015) or WordPress (WordPress 2015) if it is within your comfort zone. For simplicity's sake, let me demonstrate how a lesson would work using a basic word processing program like Microsoft Word.

If I was creating an eBook lesson for a tablet, I would start with a new word document. Rather than write out the how-tos you have just read, you must illustrate them. Don't just list the parts of an iPad; insert a diagram into your document. Provide a link to a video demonstration. YouTube is an excellent source of bite-size lessons. Different people learn in different ways. You should allow staff to read, see, and hear the same content.

When I train staff in this method, I commonly use YouTube as a source for demonstrations on how to connect to Wi-Fi, change settings, and use touch gestures. Whenever you use a video, ensure that the information is accurate— try it yourself first! YouTube also has a very useful "playlist" feature. A playlist is simply a series of videos you collect, which then play back to back. So if you were explaining several different features in "settings," you could make a playlist that went over Wi-Fi, then security, and then screen lock. To assemble a playlist, you would need to create a free YouTube account (YouTube 2015).

Once you have covered the basics of the device, it is time to instruct staff on the use of the service itself. Part of your curriculum should have involved navigating the service's "help" section. If it is an effective tool, you can rely on it to walk staff through the process of creating an account, navigating the collection, checking out, and instructing how to use an item and how to return one. Again, the key is to make it as visual as possible. If the help portion of a service is inadequate, use screenshots on a device to demonstrate the process. While it can be time-consuming, this upfront investment will save you time in the long run. A device-specific demonstration for staff can also be re-used in library handouts and web content for patrons.

Once we have completed our lesson, you should save it as a PDF (Microsoft Office 2015). This will allow you to distribute it without worrying about accidental changes to the document. We will now move on to the assembly of a training station.

The Training Station

A training station doesn't need to be complicated. At its core are an Internet-connected computer or laptop and the devices you are training on. The computer requirements are fairly basic. It will need to run a supported version of Windows. It should have a current version of a popular web browser, such as Chrome, Internet Explorer, or Firefox. You'll want to have basic peripherals, namely, a keyboard and mouse. It is advisable to also supply an on-ear headset.

An on-ear headset can easily be covered or the covers themselves can be replaced inexpensively. This is a far more hygienic option than ear buds! Headphones will also minimize noise, which is helpful if training is taking place in a shared office rather than an assigned room or if there are multiple stations.

Regarding devices, we must now consider security. Unfortunately, staff theft of mobile devices is a possibility. Even without ill intent, a staff member may move an item, causing it to go missing. As a result, you may want to consider investing in some device security. Very quickly, device security can become expensive. You need to weigh the cost of security against the likelihood of it being stolen. A high-end mount may cost two or three times as much as the tablet it is protecting!

Take into account time and opportunity. Ideally, the training station saves you time and money by giving you user-directed training, without assigning a staff trainer at all times. This can make it difficult to keep track of who is using the station at a given time. Is it in an office trafficked by staff? Is it an area you can exercise some control over with a locked door or security camera? With enough passive security, you may not even need to invest in hardware. If, on the other hand, conditions allow for too much opportunity for loss, you should probably purchase some device security.

Companies like Maclock offer some relatively inexpensive options. Some of the lowest costs are tethers. A typical one will come with a cable, a glue-on locking plate, and a key to detach the cable from the plate. These plates can be popped, but it will take quite a bit of pressure and would likely damage the device, making for a good deterrent. This system should be checked from time to time to inspect for damage. More secure (and expensive) options include enclosures, which are locking cases that are mounted on a swivel or platform. These platforms are usually drilled into a table, wall, or the ground. You often see this type of security used for point-of-sale kiosks. With regards to a staff training station, this level of security is probably unnecessary.

At this point, we have nearly all that we need. Your basic setup should be a computer on a table/workstation. On this computer, you will place PDF copies of each lesson on the desktop. Name the files accordingly: Kindle Fire, iPad, Android tablet. You have your devices you'll be training on, which are either tethered to your station or simply placed there. This station should resemble Figure 1.1. We now need to create and display some account credentials.

Recalling the open-house training, we create some demo accounts for our services. In addition to dummy accounts for services, each device will need its own proprietary account info. For example, you'll need to create an iTunes account for an iPad and a Google account for an Android device. In no case should you link these accounts to your organization's credit card! In the event that you must provide a credit card (this option has largely gone away), use a gift card. Linking a 20-dollar Visa gift card to a device means that even if

Figure 1.1 A simple training station. Lesson plans for each device are saved to the computer's desktop. Photo by Sara Roye.

the account is compromised, your organization's liability will not exceed the value of the gift card.

During the course of training, staff will need access to these accounts to install apps, change setting, and so forth. Label the back of each device with the username and password. You should also place a label with the device's name. Do not assume staff can differentiate a Kindle from an iPad, more likely, a Kindle eReader from a Kindle Fire. If staff members are using dummy accounts, you may also want to prominently display a photocopy of these library cards. A laminated copy should hold up well. Our station now complete, we should focus on the process of using device-centric training!

Running the Training Station

Once again, we must create a staff proficiency chart. We'll need the names of the staff to be trained, arranged by the department. We'll also need to list the devices they'll be training on. In this column, you can add the date each staff member "passed" their training, along with the initials of the trainer. We'll discuss this process a bit later. This document can be as simple as a printout placed on a clipboard to a cloud-based worksheet (such as a Google Doc). Table 1.1 illustrates a basic arrangement of this data.

Table 1.1 A basic staff proficiency chart. Created by Sara Roye.

Sample eBook Service								
Department	**Device**							
Name	iPad		Kindle Fire		Android		NOOK	
	Date	Trainer	Date	Trainer	Date	Trainer	Date	Trainer
James B.	12/8/2015	NT						
Sara F.								
Blake R.	12/7/2015	SB						

Once you've assembled your roster, you must next notify staff of the training requirement. As a requirement, it should come from a supervisor. This notification should tell staff the following:

What the Training Is What's the service they'll be training on?

Why It Is Necessary It is easy to forget to include the "why." "Because it's your job!" is certainly tempting, but giving a good reasoning can really be beneficial. Digital collections can be a source of great discomfort for the staff who struggle with technology. Helping them see this as an opportunity to gain confidence in their job can make them more willing participants.

Where It Is Located Is the training taking place in an office or another room? Do they need to get a key or otherwise be let in?

What Is Their Responsibility How do they complete training? With user-directed training, full-time staff members likely have flexibility to make time for themselves. Part-time staff, however, will need to make arrangements with their supervisor so as not to impact desk coverage.

What Is the Deadline Without a firm deadline, training can drag out, sputter, and die. Exceptions can always be made if there are legitimate reasons—but those are determinations that are made by a supervisor.

Where to Go to for Questions/Help When should staff seek out a supervisor? When should they seek out their trainer? Let them know the conditions for each and provide contact information.

Let's pull all these elements together. Below is a sample letter/e-mail modeled after an eBook training notice I have used in the past. References to the "road test" will be discussed shortly.

Mobile Devices and Our eBook Collection

A Hands-On Training Course
In recent years, there has been an explosion in the use of mobile devices by our public. Increasingly, the Web is being accessed not only by computers, but also by smartphones and tablets. To increase your comfort in assisting patrons as they borrow library digital material or otherwise interact with the library using mobile devices, we have created a hands-on training course.

Training will begin on month/day/year. The course consists of a training station with six devices, located in the IT Office. Corresponding instructional material, in print and video, is available in the station. Staff will be able to access the station during their work shift and learn the basics of each device at their leisure, provided they finish by month/day/year. Devices can be explored in any order. Part time staff will be afforded time to train.

How Do I Complete Training?

At any time, staff who become comfortable with a device may schedule a road test. This involves contacting a member of Digital Services, either Trainer 1 (contact info) or Trainer 2 (contact info). We will set up a time for you to complete a short list of exercises demonstrating your familiarity with a particular device:

- Understanding the basic controls
- Understanding settings, particularly Wi-Fi
- Knowledge of the device's app store (if applicable)
- Comfort with the operating systems

As a final exercise, you will also need to locate the appropriate help page for the device on the eBook help site. You may use the set of instructions to successfully download an eBook. Digital Services staff will then mark you complete on that device, and you can move on to the next one. Progress will be kept on a Google spreadsheet visible to you, your supervisor, and Digital Services staff. Once you have finished road tests for all six devices, you will have completed the training course and will receive a completion certificate, indicating your knowledge of mobile devices and the library's eBook collection.

What If I'm Having Trouble with the Course?

Full-time staff can schedule one-on-one assistance with a member of Digital Services during their off-desk hours. Part-time staff should speak to their supervisor to arrange for the same.

Before sending a letter like this, the content should be cleared by the department supervisor if they are not themselves the trainer. At my organization, I serve as a staff trainer in a stand-alone department. As a result, when I write up the above letter, I revise it with input from the department head and then have them act as the sender. The deadline you set should be ambitious but achievable. This requires that you have the pulse of the department. Generally, the scope of the lesson I outlined requires one hour per device. Obviously, someone who is already proficient with a given mobile device will not require nearly as long. The number of staff to be trained and the number of training stations you provide should also be taken into account.

The Training Begins!

Once the lesson notifications go out and the start date for training arrives, what will this process look like? Here, group dynamics can come into play. As you may recall with our open house, there was an active revision process. Print materials were altered according to feedback.

Issues with a particular service may arise with expanded use. No matter your preparation, there is always the chance that you'll need to similarly make changes to your training station. At the same time, staff will share their training experience with one another. Ideally, you want to create an early positive buzz.

With this in mind, you would do well to encourage some staff to be early adopters. Supervisors are fairly invested in the process, plus it makes sense for them to lead by example! Staff members who generally have a positive outlook can likewise benefit the group with their participation. In this way, issues that may arise with the station can be used to improve it, rather than have early mishaps serve to discourage staff.

In order to accommodate different learning styles, allow staff the flexibility to either self-direct their training or receive in-person assistance from another. As staff proficiency will be assessed by a trainer, there is a quality assurance no matter how these skills are learned. Offering self-directed training will have the added benefit of easing staffing requirements, as a trainer's presence will not be necessary at all times. Let's examine these approaches more closely.

Self-Directed Training

For self-directed training, staff will arrange time to spend at the station. Once there, they will choose a device and open the lesson you've placed on the desktop of the computer. From there, they will follow along with it, repeating the exercises on the corresponding device. Once comfortable using the device, they will focus on using the library digital collection with it, putting to use the dummy accounts you've created.

Staff-Assisted Training

In the event that a student needs a greater level of hand-holding, they will contact the trainer to set up an appointment. If the workload on your trainer/trainers becomes too great, consider utilizing staff who complete lessons early. By training the trainer, you can ease the burden on particular staff, have staff overall more actively engaged in the process, and often shorten the amount of time it takes to train a department.

When Staff Finish

In both cases, staff will reach the end of their lesson. At this point, they should contact a trainer to take their road test. A road test is simply a hands-on demonstration by the student of the core principles of each device. Let's use the iPad and an eBook service as an example.

Taking the iPad, you would turn it off and hand it to a staff member. They would be asked to turn it on and connect it to Wi-Fi. Then you would ask them to go to the app store and find and install an app, before ultimately deleting it. Have them go to a web page of their choice (within reason—some of us filter for a reason!) and create a bookmark. Once they have completed these device-specific tasks, they must move on to the digital services. In this case, that means using the iPad to successfully download an eBook.

Let Them Cheat!

For this portion of our road test, you should let staff cheat. By cheat, I mean allow them to access the eBook service's help section or the help resources your organization may have assembled. Having just trained staff, you may be tempted to have them do this portion from memory. In practice, however, your staff will likely look to use these resources when helping patrons. As the help site is usually the most up-to-date source of information, it is actually a good practice to check often. It is far more important that staff members know how to use the most common devices and be able to locate the how-to instructions on individual services.

Once a staff member has demonstrated they can effectively use both the service and corresponding device, the trainer should date and initial their proficiency chart. That staff member can move on to the next device. If they have shown real comfort with a particular device, consider using them to train other staff who may need one-on-one assistance. Once a staff member has passed their road tests on all devices, they are done! At my library, I have found that staff members do enjoy receiving a completion certificate. This is a low-cost way to reward staff for a job well done. Depending on continuing education/professional development requirements, it can also have very practical applications!

Advantages of Device-Centric Training

The benefits of device-centric training are many! They are as follows:

Time Saved

With this method of training, staff members need only train as long as it takes for them to demonstrate mobile proficiency and a basic understanding of your digital collection. If a staff member already owns a device personally, they can simply take the time to learn the digital services before scheduling a road test. When a staff member trains on a new service that is compatible with a device they've already learned, you will be able to get results with far less investment in time. Likewise, when staff is retraining annually, they should be able to move fairly quickly.

Minimal Disruption

With an upfront investment in time, the station will allow you to schedule training around desk shifts. It can be done incrementally. Pulling large numbers of staff into a training session can be difficult to work out. Large classes often mean an impersonal, lecture-style format. Not all staff members are comfortable learning in this setting. The device-centric approach I described will have the benefit of a relaxed environment, individualized help for those who need it, and a hands-off approach for those who can do without. Staff members enjoy being able to direct their training and schedule their own exam.

Relies on Traditional Reference Skills

Some librarians who may not be comfortable with technology may also be your strongest reference librarians. Reference librarians embrace the mantra "I don't know but I'll find out." This training gives them a level of comfort with the devices they'll encounter. It shows them the help site or other sources of accurate information on your digital collection. Once you've removed the mobile technology barrier, they can apply their skill at finding referral information. Simply put, they'll know how to use the Kindle Fire a patron has brought in and know where the setup information for your eBook service is located.

Training Accurately Resembles Help They'll Give Patrons

When a patron seeks help using a library digital collection, this assistance often starts with the device and not the service. In cases where staff members are showing rather than telling, they may need to turn on a patron's tablet. They will need to connect it to the library's Wi-Fi network. They may need to locate and download an app. Throughout this process, they will use the touch gestures your training station taught them. When it comes to setting up the service, they will know where the help resources are located and match them to the device they have in hand.

Training Has a Longer Shelf Life

Digital collections are subject to constant change. Supported file formats may come and go. The lending and download process evolves over time. The sites and associated apps for these services constantly change. When your focus is primarily on the service, changes like these can prove very disruptive. Some staff may even require complete retraining! This is not to say that devices do not undergo changes of their own. Since the invention of the iPhone in 2007, the iOS system has gone through versions 1 through 8 (The Verge 2013). In particular, iOS 7 had some dramatic visual changes. Overall, however, the core curriculum that was covered in the training station was actually left relatively unscathed! Instead, these updates to the operating system added new features and functionality while retaining the basic ones.

With your training focused on devices and their operating systems, you can absorb these changes in stride. Recall that our service portion of the training relies on learning how to locate and navigate help resources. When a service changes, your vendor's help site is also updated and you should move to quickly update any staff-maintained resources. In this way, your staff will always be referring to accurate information as they assist patrons on devices that they have a fair degree of familiarity with!

LAYER THREE: THE EXPERTS

So far, we've created two levels of staff knowledge around our digital collection. You have a broad base of staff that are aware of your offerings and in some cases may be using it personally. With your training station, you have assembled a front line that can assist a patron with the setup, use, and basic troubleshooting of your collection. Your first level will direct patron inquiries to your second level. These two levels will be sufficient for the vast majority of your interactions with patrons. Inevitably, situations arise that have not been addressed in training. In some cases, an error occurs that is fairly rare in nature. It could be a software glitch or human error. Other times, a device walks through the door that staff has no experience with. In these cases, a third level of assistance can come into play. I refer to this third level as your experts.

Ultimately, experts are created by both nature and nurture. On the nature side, some staff members are naturally proficient in using technology. They may own one or several mobile devices, from tablets and smartphones to eReaders. You should identify frontline staff members that demonstrate the most comfort in assisting patrons with your digital collection. A person who is naturally comfortable with technology is unflustered when a new device walks through the door. They may be unfamiliar with it; however, they intuitively grasp how it works or can quickly figure it out. On the nurture side, there are staff members who may not be tech experts but can become one with investment in time and opportunity. These are your fast learners. In either case, when you select a staff member for this third level of patron assistance, you are making it a primary function of their job. To become and remain an "expert" a staff member should do the following:

Maintain Staff Help Resources

As your existing services change, your experts should have a hand in updating any staff-maintained resources. This means FAQs, walkthroughs, print materials, and web content.

Act as a Point Person for Serious Problems/Issues

When frontline staff is truly stumped, your experts should take over. When they have solved the problem, they should communicate the answer to their coworkers and update the aforementioned resources. Even if frontline staff is able to handle a question, if it was particularly grueling, it should be passed on to your experts for future reference. Your experts can also be the ones to log help tickets with your vendors. Having an established relationship with a vendor can lead to quicker response times and better results. When your experts continually encounter the same problems, it may be time for them to push your vendors for changes to their service!

Network with Other Experts

If your library is part of a consortium, there should be opportunities to attend professional meetings on the various digital services that you offer. If you are a stand-alone library, or if your consortium doesn't offer meetings, your expert(s) should take an active role in creating them. Professional meetings offer the chance to share and address those uncommon glitches, errors, and so forth, that can arise. Rather than have individuals be stumped each time, the collective expertise in these meetings can preempt this situation. A monthly meeting of the minds is basically a knowledge multiplier for your experts!

Take Advantage of Continuing Education Opportunities

Conferences and workshops can be excellent sources of information and skill building. These can also be expensive. If the funds for regular attendance at conferences do not exist, think of more informal ways to stay abreast of technology. Allowing a staff member an occasional trip to the electronics store for some hands-on time is a low-cost solution. Here, your expert can try out the newest tablets and mobile devices. If they discover the experience to be radically different from what you've trained them on, they can adjust your curriculum to match.

FINAL THOUGHTS

Using the techniques I outlined, you have created three levels of trained staff. In each case, the investment in time is relative to their responsibility with your digital collection. For staff expected to simply know of the collection (and hopefully use it personally!), a short, open-house orientation once a year will suffice. For frontline staff, a more robust, hands-on training is required. These staff members are thus prepared for the 95 percent of patron encounters with your digital services. Finally, for your experts, their training essentially becomes a function of their job. It is ongoing. These experts will serve as your trainers going forward.

Just as we scaled our training according to need, so too should you scale your user-directed stations. If the number of people to be trained is low, you can likely get by with a single station. You can also minimize the need for multiple stations by staggering your training among departments. A station need only be as robust as you are comfortable with. The PDF lesson plan that was outlined, though it lacks all the bells and whistles of a WordPress site, works just as well.

To ensure the sustainability of your training model, upkeep is key. By keeping proficiency charts, you can ensure that staff is trained regularly. For the most part, staff will recertify annually. In the case of your experts, their immersion in library digital media is their training. With your well-trained staff, you can address the next key to a successful digital collection—patron instruction.

Chapter 2

Patron Instruction

You have trained your staff on using your digital collection so that they can assist library patrons. You must now decide on what form that assistance will take. Of course, you will help patrons over the phone and in person as questions arise. How should these interactions be structured? Beyond assistance at your reference desk, what more can you offer your public? As we noted with staff instruction, everyone learns differently. When you are instructing patrons, you must similarly offer a range of ways to learn and grow comfortable in using library digital media.

When you are considering how to make the most of your digital collection, a simple guiding principle is "make it easy." This means removing as many obstacles to using the collection as is practical. In light of that, this chapter is dedicated to offering a series of ways to make using your digital collection easier for your public. I will list the tried methods we have used at the Mastics-Moriches-Shirley Community Library (MMSCL) to great success. It will be organized according to the investment in time each method represents, starting with the lowest.

PASSIVE APPROACHES

You may be thinking that help for your patrons begins at a reference desk. Even before a patron reaches your desk, there are ways to offer instruction passively, meaning without active staff intervention. When your library takes on a new digital collection, you create posters and flyers. You list the service on your website. These first points of contact are where instruction begins.

Let's take a look at a poster/flyer. The ideal poster or flyer is 50 percent instructional and 50 percent promotional. Too often, the emphasis is placed on how great a service is and why you should use it, excluding entirely how it can be used. Take a library streaming video service, for example. While you should of course emphasize the selling points: "It's free! The titles are great!" your print materials should also list the following under a "how does it work" section.

Print Materials and Website

How Does It Work?

Step 1: Go to mylibrarywebsite.net and click on "digital collection."
Step 2: Create a free account.
Step 3: Check out and download movies.
Step 4: Watch movies on your computer, using the iOS or Android app.

In general, you should have no more than five steps. If you're doing too much explaining on a flyer/poster, patrons are unlikely to read it all. Even worse, that much text may make a service look too complicated and act as a deterrent. Finally, your print materials should always mention where to get additional help. On your website, you could list much of the same information. You could obviously drop the reference to the web page that patrons had already navigated to, but the rest of the description is applicable.

If these passive approaches resemble the first level of staff training, they should! These resources are essentially the directional information that most library staff members are trained and allowed to give patrons. For patrons who are comfortable with technology, listing a few how-tos on your print materials and website are all they need to get started. If you ignore these basics, you are simply inviting confusion and creating a barrier to access. Additionally, you are creating a larger help queue at your reference desk instead of offering an adequate first line of help!

STANDARD REFERENCE DESK INTERACTIONS

Your standard reference desk interactions are the typical walk-ins, phone calls, and e-mail inquiries you may receive. Depending on your service offerings, they may also include text messages and chat. In order to best help patrons using any of these approaches, the following resources should be made available at your help/reference desk:

Flyers

We've outlined the instructional portion each flyer should contain. When a patron approaches the desk with a basic question regarding a service, a flyer is a great way to give him the basics. Oftentimes, a patron may approach the desk without the device he intends to use the service on. In this scenario, you are providing him the simple how-tos, with the flyer pointing him in the direction of more substantial help if he needs it.

Devices

Access to the various mobile devices the staff trained on is extremely helpful when assisting the public. Devices should be secured in a locked drawer or safe. They can also be tethered to a desk. Previously, we mentioned that a patron may inquire about a service without the device she owns in hand. Having one available will allow you to briefly demonstrate the service. In the event that the interaction is taking place over the phone, it can be extremely difficult to guide a patron using a device that you don't have access to! With the understanding that it may not be feasible to have devices available at your reference desk, ensure that you provide access to robust help resources.

Help Resources

Staff training materials can often make good resources for patrons with some slight revisions. For example, when we created our staff training station, we made a series of walkthroughs for using eBooks with Microsoft Office, Blogger, WordPress, or another editor. Even if you decide not to make these the first choice for your general public audience, do make them available, maybe through a bibliography or "for more assistance" resource list. I cannot overstate how helpful these can be!

In the case of phone-based tech assistance, a robust help page can serve in place of an actual device. If you have multiple screenshots and clear instructions, you can lean on this material to guide a patron over the phone. If you are handling web-based inquiries, these materials can be e-mailed, texted, or otherwise conveyed to your patron. As you are constantly updating this content, you can provide consistently good information with a high degree of accuracy.

With these resources you can effectively assist a patron in person, over the phone, web, and so forth on the basic setup and the use of your digital services or give her a starting point. While this will deal with your patrons' immediate needs, they will likely have other questions. Your patrons are often in a situation where they don't know what they don't know. While you are doing your best to guide them, there is no perfect substitute for in-person help. Using classroom instruction, you can provide your patrons with a group setting where they can learn more, getting answers to questions they had not thought to ask.

CLASSROOM INSTRUCTION

Classroom instruction can allow you to expand the use of your digital collection, creating entire groups of new users at a time. Some patrons prefer group settings to an interaction at your reference desk, so offering both will allow you to attract a wider swathe of your public. Before we offer service-specific classes for our patrons, recall our approach to staff training. When we trained our frontline staff, I demonstrated the importance of first getting the staff acquainted with the devices they'd most likely interact with. In the same fashion, I encourage you to offer classes on mobile devices as a precursor to ones on accessing the library's digital collection.

Why Classes on Mobile Devices?

In my experiences of teaching library patrons how to access our digital collection of eBooks, movies music, and so forth, I often found my students struggling with the use of their device. They were unsure of how to connect to Wi-Fi, how their app store or market worked, and other basic features. In some cases, a patron would appear after the holidays, new iPad still in shrink-wrap, ready to download a library movie! While cases like this may seem extreme, they are far from uncommon. The question we must ask is how can patrons be expected to successfully use a library's digital collection if they cannot use the device they're navigating it with? To get your public comfortable with using the library's digital collection, you must first lay the groundwork for building their mobile competency.

I will next outline a series of tablet classes you can offer to your patrons. These classes act as a precursor to using the library's digital collection. I'll discuss curriculum, format, setup, and execution. Following that, I'll demonstrate how you can then tie them into the use of the library's applicable services!

What Types of Classes Should You Offer to Your Patrons?

Much like our staff training, our patron instruction should focus on the most common devices and operating systems that are used to access your services. You can, of course, offer training on other devices; just keep in mind these patrons will be unable to obtain library digital materials on them. Generally speaking, you should offer classes on iOS, Android, Kindle Fire, and potentially, Windows Tablets. In some cases, a class may be broken into two or more sessions focused on a common theme. Below are some classes you can offer to your patrons.

Primary Classes

These classes *must* be among those you offer your public. They will cover the minimum a patron will need to know as a prerequisite to using the library's digital collection.

iPad Basics In this class, the focus is on imparting a basic working knowledge of the iPad. Go over the basic layout of the device. You should cover simple navigation, including touch gestures. Go over how to use the Safari web browser and install and remove apps and basic settings (Apple 2015d).

Kindle Fire Basics Go over how to use touch gestures and the Fire's anatomy (Amazon Device Support 2015). Explain the basics of using Silk (the Kindle's web browser) and common settings. Go over downloading materials, from apps to media, and how to access them. In particular, you'll want to explain the basics of cloud versus device storage. Include a brief explanation of the Fire's carousel feature, where recently accessed content appears.

Android Tablet Basics As I'll explain shortly, an Android class can become a bit complicated to execute. Android has a substantial market share, however, and must not be ignored. As with all basic tablet classes, you'll demonstrate touch gestures and basic settings. The default web browser in an Android tablet may vary, so you may recommend the installation of Google Chrome (2015) for consistency's sake. This can be done when going over the installation/removal of apps.

Secondary Classes

These classes are intermediate ones that are not prerequisite to using the library's digital services, but can build further comfort. They are as follows:

All about Apps The name "all about apps" is an umbrella covering iOS, Android, and Kindle Fire. In practice, you will break these into distinct classes taught separately. The keys to each are, of course, the use of each proprietary market of apps, namely, Apple's App Store, Android's Google Play, and the Fire's Amazon App Store. Students are taught how to browse, search, and locate an app. Often, we use this opportunity to have them download the community library's mobile app (MMSCL 2014). Other options include apps used to access library digital media that may suffer from low awareness, such as our eMagazine service, Zinio. They are shown ways of assessing an app prior to download, such as understanding reviews and app permissions. You should go into app settings, discussing how you can enable and disable certain features. How apps can be updated and the process of automating this are also key.

All about iCloud In this class, the focus is on how a patron can access all their photos, music, and apps across Apple devices. You should teach how to back up an iPad/iPhone and the way to track down a missing one.

Optional Classes

These classes are ones you can offer if resources allow.

iPhone Basics The iPhone runs the same operating system as the iPad. In addition, you of course have the ability to make phone calls. As such there are several features that become applicable, such as "do not disturb" settings that you would cover in addition to the iPad Basics curriculum. In terms of using library digital media, these differences mean nothing. Here's where you must assess your organization's situation. If your goal is simply to prep patrons for use of the library's digital collection, or if you simply lack the resources to offer two separate but similar classes, you should combine the two into an iPhone/iPad basics.

Windows In addition to being a widely adopted operating system for the PC market, Windows now runs many mobile devices from phones to tablets. Its adoption rate, however, remains low and the variety of devices it is located on can compound running a class. Unless there is a demonstrated need by your public, instruction can take place on a one-on-one basis that I'll outline later. If you intend to teach a class, you should cover the same core principles we outlined, namely, basic settings, touch gestures, using Internet Explorer, and finding/downloading apps.

Preparing for a Mobile Device Class

Once you determine which classes you will be offering your public, your attention should turn to preparing to host them. Your preparations should begin with writing the program copy you'll use in your newsletter, posters/flyers, calendar, and so forth. This copy should outline the scope of each class, namely, what participants will learn. If it is an intermediate class, it should also mention any prerequisites there might be. For example, students in an All About iCloud class should have either taken iPad Basics or be familiar with the standard operation of their iPad. This will avoid unnecessary interruptions and keep the class on point. Another prerequisite is, of course, the patron's own mobile device! When you ask them to bring it, be sure to mention that it should be up to date. By up to date, we are referring to the operating system, not the device itself. Let's look at the standard copy for an iPad Basics class:

> Bring your iPad and learn how to make the most of it! Topics covered in the class include basic navigation, using the Web, and installing/removing apps and basic settings. Please make sure your iPad's operating system is up to date.

In this copy, we've done our sales pitch, informed the patrons of the scope, and indicated they need to own an iPad as a prerequisite. Regarding the up-to-date text, notice we did not mention what version of iOS. In the fast-changing world of technology, it is best to use a general term rather than specifically name a release that is superseded before the class!

Setup for a Mobile Device Class

Once we have advertised a class, we must of course move to execution. A proper program setup is among the most important elements of any class. Done correctly, it will facilitate the learning process for your students. Conversely, an ill-conceived layout can result in interruptions, frustration, and an overall unsuccessful class. With that in mind, what are the key elements of an ideal program setup?

Staff-to-Patron Ratio When conducting a class, you should aim for five to seven students per staff member. In classes we conduct at the community library, we register 15 patrons and assign 2 staff members. One staff member acts as a lead instructor, who teaches the class from the front of the room. A second staff member is a facilitator, walking around the room and assisting anyone who needs help. In a hands-on environment, it may be difficult to work with a group much larger than this.

Room Setup As patrons will be seated and going hands-on with their mobile device, you should of course have tables and chairs. As depicted in Figure 2.1, your tables should be arranged in a U-shape with the curve of the U furthest from your lead instructor. At the front of the room should be a projector screen or Smart Board.

Materials You'll provide handouts for each participant, detailing the principles you're teaching. This can be quickly assembled as it is based largely on the same curriculum you have used in your staff training. You'll also want to have flyers detailing any library service or collection compatible with the device you're instructing the class on. Finally, it can be instructive to provide attendees with a questionnaire assessing the class and instructor.

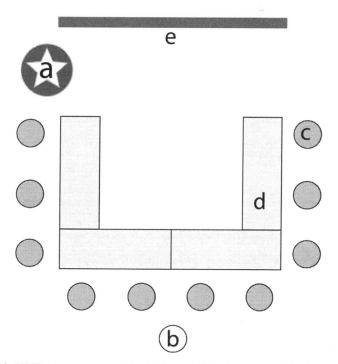

Figure 2.1 (A) The instructor. (B) The facilitator. (C) Patrons seated in chairs. (D) Tables arranged in a U shape. (E) Projector screen or Smart Board. Photo by Sara Roye.

Equipment Your instructor should have the same mobile device that you are training the class on. Additionally, you should have the appropriate VGA adapter so that you can connect your device to a projector or Smart Board. Also helpful, but not necessary, are a few styli. A stylus will allow you to touch a patron's tablet during demonstrations without actually touching it. Some patrons can be touchy (pun intended) about someone else handling their device. A stylus has the added benefit of allowing you to show a patron a concept on her device without your hand or forearm obstructing her view. In a similar vein, an inexpensive laser pointer can also be used in conjunction with your projector to draw attention to a point on the screen.

Running a Mobile Device Class

As your patrons arrive and you check them in, ensure that they have brought their devices. In a basics course, you may need to make sure that they have in fact brought the correct device! Additionally, check that they are running the current version of the device's operating system. If they are missing a major release, there will likely be quite a bit of difference between the instructor's screen and theirs. Unfortunately, these updates can take 30 minutes or more to install, meaning they may not be able to download it prior to class. In cases of no device, the wrong device, or the wrong operating system, you can provide a library device (if this is an option), have the patrons audit the class, or have them attend a future one.

When the class begins, the lead instructor (located at the front of the room) will introduce himself and the facilitator (located at the back of the room). The lead instructor should outline the format of the class, including what will be covered and how to ask for assistance: "Raise your hand and Jim will come to you." This will help prevent the entire class from grinding to a halt if an individual falls behind. The class can either follow along, using your handout, or watch on your screen/Smart Board. As the instructor goes over a topic, the students are encouraged to try each process on their own devices. Throughout the class, your facilitator should walk to the back of the room and act proactively to keep students from falling behind.

During the course of your lesson, you will find some topics taking more time than you had anticipated. Perhaps individuals are finding a concept difficult to understand. On the other hand, a particular feature may spark a lot of interest among the group. In either case, you must be prepared to advance the class along so that your core concepts are covered. When you begin to fall behind, indicate that you are moving on to the next portion of the lesson but will revisit the topic at the end of class, time permitting.

Typically, a class will run between one and one-and-a-half hours. In my experience, there can be diminishing returns as a class moves beyond the one-hour mark. Generally, it is good practice to book your room for an hour and a half, but keep your lesson to an hour. Additional time can be used to go over a topic in greater detail or cover items that are beyond the scope of the basics class.

Ending a Class

When a class approaches the end, there are a few finishing touches that can really add to its effectiveness. Consider the digital services and collections that your library offers, which are compatible with the device you just taught. You should have already assembled flyers on these items. Give a five-minute sales pitch on your digital collection. Hand out flyers to any patron who seems particularly interested. Inform attendees of any other upcoming classes that may be of interest, such as the service-oriented programs I'll discuss next. Offer one-on-one tech appointments to any patron who requires one in order to get started on a new service you just showed her. One-on-one assistance is also an option for any patron who feels he needs additional help with his device in a more personalized setting. This chapter will discuss the elements of one-on-one assistance shortly. As patrons leave your class, give them an instructor/class evaluation form that they may fill out and return anonymously.

Evaluating a Class

After the class ends, and before the next one begins, an evaluation should occur. An evaluation allows you to document any issues that may have come up. These shouldn't be viewed as failures! There is room for improvement in any class. When evaluating a class, take note of the following:

Technical Difficulties

Technical difficulties can be the scourge of any program. In one based in technology, however, the disruption can be amplified. How did your wireless network perform? Was it up to the task? You may find that having 10 or more patrons connecting their devices to your network in the same room resulted in sluggish Internet speeds. Perhaps signal strength was a problem. If your library uses a captive portal (a pop-up Wi-Fi agreement page), was it an issue? Some mobile devices can have problems processing the captive portal, leaving a patron unable to connect to your Wi-Fi.

Outside of Wi-Fi, did the device you taught with work correctly? If you used a projector or Smart Board, with a connected device, was the experience a good one for both the instructor and the audience? Perhaps a longer VGA cable could have made it easier to present. Make note of both major and minor issues.

Problems with Format

Even if you were able to avoid any technical difficulties, paper can fail you all the same. Were your handouts well received? Was the font large enough for older people or those with visual impairments? How clear were the instructions? Was there a certain point in the lesson that proved confusing? Perhaps there was a better order in covering your topics?

Improving Your Classes

Between your instructor's notes and feedback from your patrons, you should have some valuable information to act on. While some problems, particularly those involving infrastructure, can be expensive, there is often a low-cost workaround. Take, for example, our issue with low signal strength. If adding a new access point isn't an option, perhaps there are environmental factors we can address. Moving the class to an area with better coverage is a simple no-cost solution! If you have a room with moveable walls, experiment with their effect on signal strength as well.

Regarding bandwidth, needs vary not just according to your class size but also according to the topic at hand. While downloading an eBook is unlikely to impact Internet speed, streaming video can place a great burden on your network. Assuming your class is engaged in this data-intensive activity, how can you manage? With a standard wireless-N access point, you can commonly expect to get 150 Mbps (Speed Guide 2014). This would allow you to handle 10–15 users engaged in streaming video before it began to degrade. A commercial model could likely handle 30–50 people streaming video at the same time, providing far more bandwidth than necessary.

If your Internet speed lags when you have a large group and are unable to upgrade your infrastructure, manage your users. Are you running another program that relies heavily on your network at the same time? Avoid that conflict. Alternatively, you can reduce the class size to ease the burden. Finally, minor tweaks to your demonstration can help. If you are instructing your class to download an app, that is a data-intensive activity. If that is a straw that breaks the camel's back—avoid it! You can cover it academically, rather than in practice, and avoid a situation.

Equipment aside, make what changes you need to the class itself. Use larger font to make it easier to read, if it proves an issue. Use less font and more illustrations if your patrons find your handouts overwhelming. If patron evaluations take issue with an instructor, conduct an audit of the class. More often than not, the problems you will encounter can be remedied through training.

By conducting mobile device classes for your patrons, you are building the prerequisite skills to using your library's digital collection. The hope is that following these classes, a portion of your patrons will immediately begin borrowing from your collection of eBooks, streaming movies, music, and so forth. What of those patrons who, while they have a working knowledge of their device, may still require a bit of help in using your digital collection? For these patrons, we will look at service-oriented programs you can offer before turning to one-on-one instruction.

Service-Oriented Classes

Simply put, a service-oriented program is a class on a specific digital collection offered by your library. As mentioned, these classes are geared toward patrons who already have a working knowledge of the device they'll be using in conjunction with the service. These classes share many similarities with mobile device instruction with some key differences. Let's look at the process of developing service-oriented classes for your patrons.

What Classes Should You Offer?

Surprisingly, this question is not as straightforward as it seems. While you will of course offer classes on the digital collections your organization has, it may be necessary to subdivide them more narrowly. For example, it may not make sense to offer a one-size-fits-all class on your library's streaming video service if the setup and use of the service varies wildly between devices. So how then should you develop them?

Identify Similar Experiences Once you list all the collections you'll be offering classes on, examine what the experience is like on each of the major devices compatible with them. Devices that share a similar experience can be taught in the same class. In identifying a similar experience, look at obtaining an app for the service, creating an account, locating materials, downloading them, and then using them. If that setup is very different on a Kindle Fire tablet versus an iPad, or if the app interface looks very different, you should teach the two separately. Writing a class handout serves as a good litmus test. If when you are creating it you find yourself making many qualifying statements (now for people using a Kindle, you don't need to download an app), that's an excellent indicator that you need to subdivide your program.

In practice, this might mean that rather than having a "Library eBooks" class, you will instead have "eBooks on Your Kindle," "eBooks on My Black and White eReader," and "eBooks on My iPad/Android" classes. Even using this narrower focus, there can be some variety. If your patron base is a large one and the program attendance numbers can justify it, you may wish to offer a wide range of service-oriented classes on individual devices, to include other eContent, such a streaming movies, or eMagazines.

Writing Your Copy

As I've pointed out, a carefully written copy not only gets your patrons interested in a program but can also ensure they are prepared for the class. Your copy should let them know what you'll be covering and what they need to bring. If a service requires an e-mail address, a library card in good standing, a piece of hardware, or an existing proprietary account (such as an Amazon account), be sure to communicate this! When doing so, avoid jargon! For example, if you have a streaming video service, call it that! Hoopla, IndieFlix, and other library video services are not synonymous with streaming video in the minds of many of your patrons. Here's a sample copy:

Free Library eBooks on Your Kindle!

We'll go over our collection of free library eBooks and how to get started borrowing them on your Kindle eReader or Kindle Fire tablet. Be sure to bring your device, library card and Amazon username/password.

What to Cover

In a service-oriented class, you can ignore most aspects relating to how a patron's device works. This is not the time to explain touch gestures or how to create an iTunes account! Depending on the structure of your class, you may have several different devices present! Patrons requiring this level of help should first attend a basics course on their device or request one-on-one help. Your service-oriented classes must be narrowly focused on your collection or they will quickly fall apart amid a flurry of device questions. At the most, you may need to guide the group through connecting to your organization's Wi-Fi network. Once your class is connected to your wireless network, you should cover the following:

General Introduction What is the service and what is its name? This should be the vernacular versus the proprietary name. "This is our eBook service, which is called Overdrive." Emphasize a few quick points that will build some interest: "This is a really great collection of popular titles." Making these emphases can be extremely important if your library offers multiple services dealing in the same media. Typically, when a library maintains two different platforms, they do not carry identical content. For example, if your library uses both Overdrive and One Click Digital for audiobooks, what are the distinguishing features? Does one have an emphasis on a particular genre or carry authors unavailable elsewhere? As long as these services don't radically differ in setup and use, they can be taught together. If, on the other hand, they provide very different experiences, consider offering a separate class for each. You can always introduce patrons to the service you leave off at the end of your class, time allowing.

Where to Find Your Collection Where is the collection located on your website? If there is an app to install, guide them through the process of locating and downloading it. If the download process is a long one, either based on the file size or the download speed at your library, you can skip ahead to navigating the collection.

Setting Up an Account Do you need to create an account? Log in with your library barcode? Is there a username/password? Is there a way for the login and/or preferences to be saved. Some will view this as a convenience, while patrons with privacy or security concerns will not.

Navigating the Collection How do you find what you're looking for? Is there a keyword search? Advanced search? How about a browse option?

Checking Out/Downloading Once you find what you're looking for, how do you get it? Is it a simple checkout process? Do you need to download the item? Depending on the type of media, it may be some combination of streaming and/or downloading. Be sure to explain this process to the patrons, as it can impact their device's data plans!

Using Their Item Once a patron has checked out and/or downloaded an item, how is it played, read, listened to, or otherwise accessed?

Settings/Features How can a patron customize his experience? If it's an eBook, how does one change the font size or color or add a bookmark? If it's a video, how to you pause, fast-forward, or rewind? Are there volume settings? Closed captioning?

Reserves, Returns Depending on the collection, digital materials might not always be available. If they are checked out, can you place a hold? If so, how is this done? Can you request an item be purchased? What is the procedure? Finally, can you return an item early? If an item expires, is it automatically removed, or is there a process that you need to show a patron?

Basic Troubleshooting While you're guiding patrons through the process of using a service, they may encounter problems at a later date. Showing them where your help resources are and how to navigate them can help alleviate frustrations. If there are some known issues, address them at this point.

Setup for a Service-Oriented Class

The setup for a service-oriented class is very similar to the mobile device ones, with a few key differences:

Staff-to-Patron Ratio

In order to come up with a number, consider the relative ease or difficulty in using a service. If the setup involves numerous steps, or if the user interface (patron side) of a service is difficult to navigate, you should probably have no more than five to seven patrons per staff member. If, on the other hand, a service is relatively simple to use and the class has more of a lecture feel, you can of course increase the size.

Room Setup

In classes where the format will involve a hands-on setup of a service, the U-shaped tables we used in our mobile device classes are appropriate. If your class takes on more of a lecture format, you will likely lose your tables in favor of several rows of chairs.

Equipment

In either a lecture format or hands-on workshop, you will need a representative device connected to a projector or smartboard. If audio is involved, make sure that your setup is appropriate to the size of your audience. This might mean a laptop's internal speakers, a set of external speakers, or even an auditorium's sound system.

Next, consider how your patrons will be using the service in class. They will be bringing their mobile devices. That being said, in some cases a service may require (or be easiest) using a computer to locate and check out materials. In cloud-based services, checked out digital items are then retrieved on the patron's tablet. If that is the case, you may need to provide a number of laptops/desktops for patron use. Your goal should be to provide an experience in class that resembles as closely as possible the experience outside of class.

Running a Service-Oriented Class

As with our mobile device classes, your setup should include a lead instructor aided by at least one facilitating staff member. As you check your patrons in prior to the start of class, assist them in connecting to your public Wi-Fi. Have your projector or Smart Board display a representative slide or image so that you can address any seating issues before starting. If a patron has difficulty seeing the screen, it is far easier to make changes in seating arrangements, room brightness, or screen size at this time than after you begin. Once everyone is seated, give your patrons any handouts they are meant to follow along with. Introduce yourself and any facilitators. Explain to attendees how they can signal for help from the facilitator if it is needed. Once you've done this, your sales pitch begins!

Why a Sales Pitch?

In your mobile device classes, there wasn't much convincing to be done. Your patrons were attending your class because they wished to know how their device operated. In a service-oriented class, your patrons are interested in consuming digital media, but they may not be sure that they want library digital media. Free is great, but is free enough? Throughout a service-oriented class, focus on engaging your audience and selling your service.

As soon as you move past the setup of a service and into navigating the collection, hit upon the selling points. Sure you'll show a canned search that you've already tested in advance. This is a great way to demonstrate the basic principles of using your service. As a means of generating excitement, however, it is somewhat lacking. Like any good salesperson, you must know your product inside and out.

Ask attendees what it is they're interested in. Tailor your approach to their interests. If you're teaching a class on an eBook service and the patrons indicate they're interested in horror, show them how to browse the horror genre. Show them an author search for Stephen King. Demonstrate an applicable advanced search. This sort of interactivity is far more engaging for your patrons than running through some examples that may or may not reflect their interests.

Understandably, this can be a bit disconcerting for an instructor. Empowering your patrons in a class means surrendering a bit of control. It requires greater preparation on the instructor's part in terms of knowing the ins and outs of the collection. It can require a bit of improvisation! While running off a strict script will ensure order, does it really mirror the patron's experience?

In any service you show, there will be strengths and weaknesses. Know them. Inform your patrons of them. "Our streaming movie service has a really great documentary selection, but it's a bit light on newer romance movies." We're not out to trick our patrons, are we? When the patrons try a digital collection, they're not entering into a contract. If they don't like the service, they'll stop using it. Better to show a collection, warts and all, and allow your patrons to make an informed decision.

To recap, make sure that as you cover the key points of a service you convey enthusiasm for the service. Use pretested searches when it is necessary to demonstrate a principle. At the same time, involve your audience and their interests when searching a collection.

Ending a Class

For service-oriented classes, schedule them to be an hour long. Forty-five minutes of your time will be used to cover all of the setup of the service and its use. Your remaining 15 minutes will allow you to address specific questions not covered in your presentation. You can also use this time to make mention of other upcoming programs or digital collections that may be of interest. In the case that a service has a glaring weakness, do you offer a complementary one? For example, if the eBook collection you just instructed patrons on has a strong fiction collection but lacks nonfiction, can you point your patrons to a high-interest collection of nonfiction eBooks?

Before your patrons leave, offer them the option to arrange one-on-one assistance on the service you have just showed or another one they may be interested in. Hand out flyers on any other compatible digital collection you offer. Finally, give your patrons a class/instructor evaluation form to be filled out and returned anonymously. We can now turn to assessment.

Evaluating a Class

When you evaluate a service-oriented class, you will look at the same basic categories we used in our mobile device classes. These were, as you recall, technical difficulties, problems with format, and ways to improve a class. While the assessment of technical difficulties is the same as in our mobile device classes, you may encounter problems with the format, which are unique to training patrons on a service.

Unlike your mobile device classes that focused on a particular model, instruction on a service may involve several different devices at a time. While you took steps to ensure the differences in experience weren't too great when developing the class, there is always a difference when theory is put into practice! Note when in your class differences between devices became most pronounced. How much confusion did it cause? How can you address it? Is it a simple matter of clearer instructions? If the disruption is great and not easily remedied, you may need to consider teaching that service and device separately.

Next, consider your sales pitch. How was it received? How can it be improved? As your sales pitch relied on a bit of improvisation, did this lead to specific difficulties? When you allowed patrons to guide a sample search of your collection, were they satisfied with the selection? Were they attempting to use the collection in a way that left them dissatisfied? Taking these things into account will allow you to better communicate before your next program, when you are writing copy, and during the class itself. These considerations, along with the feedback you receive from your evaluation sheets, will allow you to continually improve upon your programs.

We have thus far looked at assisting patrons at the reference desk in person, over the phone, and via e-mail and other means of communication. We have examined mobile device classes you can offer to increase your patron's digital literacy prior to using your digital collections. Finally, we have worked through how to develop and execute service-specific classes for your public. We will now look at developing a model for one-on-one patron tech help.

ONE-ON-ONE PATRON INSTRUCTION

Exactly What Is One-on-One Tech Help?

One-on-one tech help is a prolonged, in-person reference interaction with a patron. Unlike standard reference questions, tech help is done on a by-appointment basis. A tech help appointment is meant to address a patron's particular technology concern. Generally, these appointments are scheduled for one-hour increments. Shortly, I will discuss defining the scope of tech help, but it should include basic device instruction and use of the library's digital services/collections.

Why Offer One-on-One Tech Help?

As discussed, everyone has different learning styles. Classroom instruction, while it can be a very effective way to teach a group of patrons how to use their device or compatible library collections, may not work for some patrons. Perhaps they are uncomfortable in a classroom setting. It is possible the times your classes occur do not allow a patron to attend. More often, a patron may require a level of hand-holding that makes classroom instruction a poor fit. Consider how disruptive one patron can be to the overall class if she continually requires individual assistance. Having the option to refer a patron to a one-on-one consultation is a lifesaver, allowing you to come back to your planned classroom content. In the case of troubleshooting a service or device, a librarian may need to do some prior research before helping. The length and depth of these interactions make them difficult to treat like a standard reference desk interaction.

Setting Up a Tech Help Service

So how do you get started offering your patrons a one-on-one tech help service? Let's examine the key elements of one:

Defining the Scope

What type of help will this service offer? It should, of course, cover the setup and use of the digital collections and services your organization offers to the public. Your library has an OPAC, allowing patrons to find materials, but surely you've discovered that not all of them are able to! It would be outrageous to think that the patron who cannot navigate your physical collection of books, movies, music, and so forth would have no recourse! As we have learned, a patron who wants to use your digital collection but is unfamiliar with the device he'll be using to do so will likely struggle. Just as you should offer classroom device instruction, individualized one-on-one help can turn a confused patron with a new device into a power user of your eContent!

Beyond device instruction and use of your services, you can define tech help more broadly, if it suits your organization. At the MMSCL, we offer assistance in using social media, video chat, common software applications, digitization of print and analog, management of digital photos, and more. Clearly, these are offerings that can build digital literacy, but are not strictly tied to the use of your library's collection.

What Equipment Do You Need?

Once you've defined the scope of the assistance you'll be offering, you can determine what equipment you'll need to facilitate. Your patrons will be bringing their own devices when you help them, but this doesn't mean you won't need access to your own! In some instances, your one-on-one tech help will require you to test and research fixes, features, and so forth. While forums can be a valuable source of information, they do not replace having the same or comparable device. As much as possible, you want to have a solution already in hand when your patron arrives rather than dabbling with his during an appointment!

As with our staff training, remember to focus on operating systems and common devices. An iPad, Android Tablet, and Kindle Fire with current versions of their operating system will prove sufficient in the vast majority of your tablet questions. As the Kindle Fire handles eBooks very similar to the Kindle eReader, the addition of a NOOK or Kobo should complete your mobile devices (unless you encounter Windows tablets on a regular basis). Of the laptops or PCs at your library, it is important to have one with the current Windows operating system. In addition to Windows, a portion of your patrons use Macs. While they are outnumbered by Windows users, you should consider purchasing a Mac if budget allows.

In addition to devices, there a few inexpensive peripherals that can prove helpful when doing one-on-one tech appointments. Occasionally, a patron may forget her charger. You, of course, will have one on hand for any device you choose to purchase. Despite this, you may wish to consider having an additional micro and mini USB charger, which will power a range of devices. An Apple lightning connector and 30-pin charger will cover old and current iOS devices. Having these on hand can mean the difference between postponing a tech appointment and simply providing an outlet to charge while you conduct one.

Staffing Requirements

As this is a by-appointment service, you will have the luxury of matching the staff to a particular patron concern. Shortly, I will go over the specifics of scheduling. In a general sense, you will require your level two (frontline staff) and level three (your experts) to cover these appointments. Your frontline staff will handle the basic setup and the use of your digital services and patron devices. Your experts, on the other hand, will stand in for more substantial questions involving troubleshooting uncommon devices and advanced features. A staff member should be assigned to the supervision of the service overall, ensuring that appointments are followed up on and done to an acceptable standard.

The Logbook

When you begin scheduling appointments, you'll need a log to record the appointments. This log will need to have several fields including the following:

Date of Interaction Not to be confused with the appointment date, this is the day the patron initially requests help. Keeping track of this will help ensure that your patrons do not wait too long for assistance and that when possible you can dispense help on a first-come, first-serve basis.

Person Recording the Request You should keep track of the person taking requests as a means of quality control. If an intake form is filled out incorrectly, you can easily identify the employee responsible and take steps to correct the situation.

Patron Contact Info This basic information should include the patron's name and phone number. E-mail can be optional, but should be in addition to a phone contact. This will prove helpful when scheduling, rescheduling, or canceling an appointment.

Topic of Appointment It would be impossible to prepare to help a patron if we didn't know the topic! When recording the topic, the more information the better. We'll go over the elements of a tech help reference interview shortly.

Date and Initials of the Librarian Returning the Call Providing this information will allow you to ensure a patron has been contacted or left a message. In the case that a patron claims there was no follow-through, you have documentation of your attempts.

Date and Initials of the Librarian Taking the Appointment When a librarian sees an outstanding tech help request, she will contact the patron and make an appointment.

Special Notes This field serves as your other category. Here, you can put information on a patron's preferences regarding time: "weekdays in the morning are best," the staff "requested that James help her," or other situation. It might contain additional information on their problem. For example, the topic of appointment might be help using your streaming music service, while your special notes explain that the patron had been using the service for a year and only recently encountered an issue.

Outcome The outcome is your final field. In it, you will record whether the appointment took place, and if so, if it was successful. If a patron makes a follow-up appointment, indicate it there in addition to adding a new entry to your log.

Creating a Logbook

Now that we know what fields should be included in a logbook, what form should it take? While pen and paper can provide an adequate record, I strongly suggest you consider using Google Forms/Google Docs (2015) for their flexibility and shared information. These products are free cloud-based services that can allow your information to be easily shared among staff members—particularly important in a multi-branch library. A Google Form is a web-based form the fields of which you can customize, in this case to the specifications above. The form can be placed on your reference desk computers and used during patron requests. The data that is entered appears on a connected spreadsheet. The person making the form then provides access (via an e-mail invitation) to the staff who will be making follow-up calls and appointments. You do have the option to embed a form on your library's website, allowing patrons to fill out the form itself. In this case, you would only include the fields that a patron would need.

Writing Your Copy

Once you have your staff in place and a logbook to record appointments, it is time to let your public know about the service! Remember to let patrons know the scope of your one-on-one tech appointments. If you are limiting the service to basic device lessons and the use of your digital services, make this apparent in your copy. Make it clear how to go about making an appointment, whether this is by going to your website, calling the reference desk, or other means. You'll want to let them know of the length of these appointments as well. In my experience, an hour is enough time to handle most concepts. Appointments lasting much longer than this begin to lose their effectiveness, as a patron can suffer from information overload. Better to schedule a follow-up appointment and let them digest what they have been taught.

At this point, you have your staff, you've created an intake form, and you've let your public know of the service. The question is, how will it work in practice? Let's examine a sample workflow.

Handling Incoming Requests

When a patron initially requests a tech appointment, you must gather the required information on your form. Your intake form does not need to have every field we just listed. In practice, your form consists of the date of the interaction, the patron's name and contact information, the nature of the problem, and any special notes. At this point, let your patron know that you will be in touch with him shortly.

Processing Outstanding Appointments

When a request appears, the next level of staff involvement begins. The staff should be keeping an eye on your log for outstanding appointments. Indeed, it would be wise to make a staff member responsible for this service as a whole. The benefit of using a Google Form for a tech appointment service is that any of your staff who have permission to access it can choose to receive alerts automatically. A staff member who chooses to receive alerts will get an e-mail that your shared document has had an addition, helping to automate your workflow. Whether you choose to use such a solution or not, patron requests must be followed upon.

Whether your appointments are assigned or voluntarily taken by a pool of staff members, you should ensure that the staff member is a good fit to the patron concern. For example, if a patron needs help with a Windows tablet and your library doesn't have one, a librarian on the staff who owns one personally would be an ideal match. From your intake form, you have a general sense of what the patron needs, but do not make assumptions! You may have a technology question being asked by a person who is unfamiliar with technology! Your next step is to return your patron's phone call.

Here's where your reference interview occurs. Restate what your patron has asked for help with and attempt to get some details. "Mrs. Smith, you said you needed some help using your iPad. What exactly are you having trouble with?" Questions like these help in a number of ways. More information will allow you to narrow the scope. Using the question above as a starting point, you may learn that the patron is having difficulty understanding how to connect to Wi-Fi. At the same time, you will also learn the patron's comfort with technology. If the response to your question is "everything," you know you are working with a beginner. In this case, you will likely plan to teach a few basic getting-started tips over the appointment. As you define the nature of the problem, you will learn whether it is even within the scope of the help you offer! Assuming it is, we can move to booking the appointment.

Booking an Appointment

Aside from the obvious where and when, you'll need to provide a few more details to your patron. Once you've gained an understanding of their problem, you should relay to them what they'll need to bring to an appointment. Aside from their device, they may need to have account information on hand. This could be the account username/password on their device, such as an iTunes or Amazon account, access to e-mail, or their library card. Ensuring they have the essentials will cut down on delays or the need to reschedule an appointment. Once an appointment is booked, you can update your log with the time, date, and staff member that is participating.

Running a One-on-One Tech Help Appointment

When your patron arrives, your instructor will introduce himself before guiding the patron to your designated area. Depending on your organization, this may be a small meeting room or an area on the public floor. Obviously, noise can present a distraction, so you should choose your space with this in mind. Noise works both ways, and the instructor and student can be disruptive to others, particularly if the concept involves audio! In addition to being quiet, your space should be within your wireless coverage, unless it is not a requirement for an individual appointment. Access to an electrical outlet will ensure battery life doesn't end your tech help prematurely. Finally, a tabletop capable of accommodating two people sitting on the same side and two chairs will complete your list of needs.

Establishing the Correct Approach

Early into your appointment, you should get a feel of your patron's comfort level with technology. To some degree, your phone conversation should give you an advance sense of it. For a patron who may struggle with technology, do your best to avoid jargon. When you need to use technical terms, take the time to define them. Pinch, stretch, swipe, and other touch gestures can confuse a patron who doesn't know what they mean. At the same time, a few moments spent explaining can reveal them to be simple concepts rather than impediments to learning.

Going over a Concept

When going over a concept, you may need to first do it yourself, then have the patron attempt the same. With the understanding that a patron is going to be repeating your instructions, break them into digestible pieces. Don't go at your usual speed; go at a pace that your patron can follow. In some cases, they'll want to write down the process. Depending on the topic, you may have referral information readily available. Using the example of getting started with your eBook service, you could show the patron your classroom or other handouts or perhaps web-based support material. For some, this will serve in place of taking notes, saving both of you time.

Whether or not you are providing notes, whenever a patron is required to make a username, pin, or password, be sure to have them record it somewhere. During an appointment, your patron absorbs a lot of information. They switch from participant to observer and actively ask questions. In this shuffle, it is easy to forget the account credentials that they have just set up! The last thing you want to do is spend additional staff and patron time engaging in account recovery!

Ending a Tech Appointment

At a certain point, you will either have finished instructing your patron on a topic or have reached the end of your allotted time. *What comes next?*

If You Were Unable to Complete a Topic If you are approaching the end of an appointment without completing a topic, consider your next step. Are you able to extend the appointment? If an extra 10 minutes will allow you to cover what is left and won't impact scheduling, then this is a good option. If this is not the case, pick a point in the process that, if not ideal, is at least practical to end on. You never want to end with an account half set up or an incomplete installation. In any process you are doing, there are likely a few waypoints you can identify as a place to stop. When you reach a waypoint, discuss with the patron whether he wishes to continue on his own or set a second appointment up.

Whenever possible, the follow-up appointment should be conducted by the same staff member. Not only will the same staff member know exactly where the appointment left off, they will already be familiar with the patron's ability and learning process. Additionally, (one hopes) they have already established a rapport with the patron. When booking a follow-up appointment, be sure to enter it into your logbook both for statistical purposes and for recording where the appointment left off. Remember, there are times when another staff member might need to fill in!

If You Completed a Topic When you've completed a topic, touch base with your patrons. Are they comfortable with the process? Is there anything they'd like you to go over again? Perhaps they have a related question. If you've just got them comfortable using a particular device, perhaps they would be interested to learn about another? Have handouts on relevant services handy. They may wish to try it out at home or schedule an additional appointment. If you have a service-based class upcoming or an intermediate tablet class, these may also be of interest.

END THOUGHTS

Using a combination of active and passive approaches, it is possible to create a robust system of support for patrons using your services. Carefully devised posters and flyers can both promote and instruct patrons simultaneously. Web-based help information can allow a patron to assist himself at home, rather than wait until he can make a trip to the library. In the case that a patron stops by your reference desk seeking assistance, the staff access to basic equipment and referral information at your reference desk helps ensure positive outcomes.

Investing in classroom instruction can vastly improve patron access to your digital collection. Device classes help create the requisite skills a patron will need in order to consume library digital media. With improved digital literacy, a patron can become a lifetime user of your digital library. For patrons with a basic understanding of how to use their personal device, service-oriented programs can quickly instruct groups on how to get started on borrowing digital media from your library.

Finally, having formalized one-on-one help available ensures you reach those needing the most assistance. Rather than lose these potential borrowers, investing the time in personalized instruction can mean gaining new users. In addition to helping high-needs patrons, one-on-one assistance allows you to effectively troubleshoot issues that may prevent a patron from beginning or continuing to use your collections. A patron who suddenly encounters a service-breaking error is a patron that isn't borrowing library materials. Imagine if your library card encountered an error at checkout and you had no recourse! One-on-one help allows you to take these (hopefully) rare issues and remedy them.

Ultimately, patron instruction is intended to remove barriers to access. If you embrace the mantra "make it easy" and use it as a guide to assisting your public, you are likely to succeed. Easy-to-use correlates to want-to-use. Examine your services and assemble simple-to-read instructions on getting started. Identify stumbling blocks and assemble helpful referral information to combat them. Have your reference desk set up with the materials and equipment needed to effectively help patrons in person, over the phone, and online. Note what devices your public uses and offer classes that will make them comfortable in using them. For patrons comfortable using their device, but not a service, utilize service-based programs to get them interested in, set up with, and use your collections.

When we discussed staff training in the previous chapter, we identified a lack of awareness as an obstacle. As we continue to seek ways of removing barriers to access, we'll examine how to market a digital collection in the next chapter!

Chapter 3

Doing Familiar Library Marketing in New Ways

Recall that when we examined staff training, the basic requirement of all employees was awareness of your digital collection. In regards to all library services, awareness is essential! A lack of staff awareness can hamstring a collection, as employees cannot properly direct your patrons to all that you offer. While the success of a collection in part relies on the staff, you must also do your best to empower your patrons. If a patron doesn't know you have specific services, it doesn't matter how good it is, how easy it is to use, or how much help you have made available—he won't use it.

In an attempt to market a digital collection, you may initially struggle to come up with ways of promoting what is an initially new and unfamiliar service. While there are innovative, technology-driven approaches to marketing that are outlined in the next chapter, they are not the only way forward. Rather, you can take familiar approaches that you have used in support of your library collections, programs, and services and apply them to your digital collection.

There are advantages to proceeding this way. By starting with the familiar, you can move with haste to create a strong base of users. Using traditional approaches to marketing may also help your library manage change. The sudden introduction of a digital collection can be stressful. If your initial marketing campaign is completely new at the outset, you may have added a second large body of new information to digest. This can unnecessarily stress the staff. What is more, you are dividing attention between learning new marketing techniques and learning a new digital service.

With this in mind, let's recall all the traditional ways we promote library services, programs, and collections. As we do, we will work to apply these techniques in the service of a digital collection. With some tailoring, much of your standard approaches to marketing will prove highly effective.

TRADITIONAL PRINT MARKETING

Print marketing, having been around for some time, is something that many libraries already do very well. Our comfort with the medium, however, can be tested when we're using it to describe the digital. Let's examine some basic elements of successful print marketing.

Posters/Flyers

Recall that in the chapter on patron instruction, we defined a successful flyer as being 50 percent promotional and 50 percent instructional. We used the instructional text as a simple method of teaching a patron to use a digital collection. In any poster/flyer that you make, be sure to include the "how does it work" elements I outlined. In addition to this portion, you must of course give the patrons a reason to use the service.

What are its selling points? Identify strengths in the content of a collection. How about mobility? Is there an app? Ease of use? This content should lead in your print materials. Briefly list them ahead of the "how does it work" elements. Finally, list the places where a patron can receive more information/help. This might be your reference desk, one-on-one tech appointments, web content, or some combination of the three. Refer to Figure 3.1 for a sample flyer utilizing these features.

Consider Utilizing QR Codes

Unlike flyers, which a patron can take home with them, a poster is a fixed advertisement which remains in-house. While you can communicate a fair amount of information with a poster, some portion of it may be lost by the time the patron gets home. QR codes are an excellent way to transmit a good deal of detail to your patrons through print advertising while taking up a very small area of space. So what exactly is a QR code? A QR code or quick response code is a two-dimensional barcode that when read by a mobile tagging app can open a web page, among other things (The Computer Language Company 2015). Simply put, if you open a scanner app on your mobile device and then scan a QR code, a web page can load.

A practical use for a QR code might be to provide a link to an app required to use a digital collection. If you had a poster advertising your Axis360, Overdrive, or other eBook collection, it could benefit your patrons to scan and be taken to download in their device's app store. If a service requires a bit more explanation on how to get started, you may instead wish to direct them to further information listed on your library's website. This might be the place where you list your digital collections in detail, frequently asked questions, or other help resources. Basically, a QR code can allow you to provide more information than a patron can commit to memory or a poster can reasonably include. It also has the added advantage of taking a mobile device directly to the source.

So how then does one get started using QR codes? Fortunately, for both you and your patrons, there are free QR code readers and QR code generators. For patrons, this scanning of a QR code will require that they download a reader. A cursory search in a device's app store should yield some good, free

Register at www.hoopladigital.com
or download the hoopla app on your iOS or Android
mobile device and click on *Sign Up*. Provide an email
address, a password, and library card information.
Find the Hoopla app in the Apple App Store or the
Google Play Store.

Begin Browsing
Click *Browse* and choose the Music, Movies, Audiobooks, or Television
tab or search for a specific title by typing in your title/keyword in the
search box.

Begin Borrowing
Click on the *Titles* icon and then click the *Borrow* button. Your
borrowed titles can be found under the *My Titles* tab for viewing/
listening. Borrowed titles will be automatically returned when
your lending period is over.

Need More Help?
For additional help visit www.hoopladigital.com and click the
Need Help? link at the bottom of the page. You can also schedule
one-on-one help with library staff by calling 399-1511 x240.

06-14

Figure 3.1 A sample flyer for a streaming movie and music service, Hoopla. Note the simple overview indicating how to access the collection, followed by where a patron may receive additional assistance. Photo by Sara Roye.

options. Your responsibility is to provide a QR code to scan. Kaywa is a free, reliable QR code generator. You simply type in the URL you wish to encode and then generate! You download the QR code, which is an image, and then add it to your poster. That's it!

Positioning Posters

Once you've assembled your posters, where do you put them? How do you get your flyers into the hands of your patrons? Starting with your posters, you'll want to identify your audience. Does it serve a particular patron base? For example, if you have a streaming music service and the content is predominantly for adults, then it may not serve to place posters in your teen area. With this in mind, you could limit your posters to areas trafficked by adults. Keep in mind your children's area is teeming with parents!

Once you've broadly identified your areas, next consider the media type. If it's a streaming video service, you may want to place a poster where your movies are located. Likewise, an eBook service should be located near the print collection. Even within a collection, some places are better than others. Let's identify some approaches!

In All Collections

In any collection, your patrons are drawn to what's new. If you separate your new releases from the rest of your collection, you have created a magnet. Take advantage of it!

Streaming Movies and/or Music

In an audiovisual collection, there are likely several hotspots. If you list upcoming releases anywhere, this might be an opportune place for a poster. It is well trafficked, and as the content is constantly changed, patrons will revisit it time and again. If you have a separate AV room otherwise requiring patrons to check out media before leaving the area, the place where the checkout line forms may be ideal. Patrons here are essentially a captive audience. Standing in line holds little excitement, and a poster detailing a streaming movie or music collection can be an informative little diversion.

eBooks

If you list the release calendar for titles, or if you display the New York Times Bestseller List, these are the places that readers are drawn to. As you know, these titles are often on a hold list. Perhaps the digital copy of the same book is available or at least has a shorter queue? Traditional book displays and bibliographies also bring in readers. Why not let these consumers of print know about their digital options!

eMagazines

Traditionally, your magazine collection is displayed cover out with the newest issue in front. As a serial, magazines are published at regular intervals, so you won't be listing new releases or otherwise curating content. In this case, examine your loan rules. Do print magazines circulate? How about new issues? If you restrict access to new or all magazines, simply modifying a poster to emphasize the advantage of the digital copy can be a strong incentive to use. Remembering that magazines are a browsed collection, locate a poster centrally. Many patrons take a magazine and then enjoy them in-house. Wherever these patrons commonly find seating would be another ideal location.

Getting Flyers into Your Patrons' Hands

Unlike posters, flyers are intended to be taken home by your patrons. Generally, a flyer has the advantage of mobility over a poster, but lacks the same visibility. How best then to get them into your patrons' hands?

Raise Their Visibility

While a stack of flyers on their own isn't much of a presence, adding it to a larger display can raise its visibility. For example, in the same way that we identified a book display as a spot to locate a poster, some flyers in an acrylic holder would also serve. If possible, flyers can serve as a complement to your poster, serving as info to go. Later, we will discuss some interactive displays, which can also be a landing spot for flyers.

Hand Them Out!

This seems obvious, but unless you wish to waste paper and annoy your public, you should probably have more of a focus. Rather than placing thousands of flyers under the windshield of everyone's cars in the parking lot, let's key in on supplying them to those most likely to want them. Recall our mobile device classes. Following the class, a short pitch on a compatible digital collection can end with patrons taking a flyer that goes into further detail. At your reference desk, if a patron inquires about a service, you should give her a flyer to take with her. This is not a substitute for talking about the service, but rather some information to go.

Think Circulation

Attaching a flyer to holds is a great way to more narrowly target your audience. Much like we placed posters advertising digital collections near their corresponding physical collection, you can similarly pair flyers to holds. For example, you can hand out a flyer to your patrons advertising a streaming music service when they pick up CDs they have on hold. If holds are picked up directly by patrons without staff assistance, you can simply attach a flyer in advance. Patrons may have some questions about an individual service— luckily, all staff members would have been trained to know the very basics!

Targeting holds allows you to focus on a material type without having to spread your attention on individual items. Obviously, it is impractical to place flyers or other print advertisements to all or even a portion of a collection. Even if you were to do so, one patron may check out several items, all containing duplicate flyers! You can have the circulation staff hand out flyers to patrons checking out particular material types in the same fashion; however, this can be thwarted by self-checkout machines.

When a patron receives a new card in person or in the mail, you should consider providing him an information packet on your digital services. This can be a collection of your flyers detailing individual services. Many libraries give new cardholders a welcome packet that includes an overview of the library. If so, consider this another destination for your flyers.

Newsletters

Print newsletters have been a staple of library marketing for a long time. A large number of your patrons look to them for information about upcoming programs, new services, library news, and so forth. Libraries are very good at placing an article in the newsletter whenever a new digital collection is added, but often neglect to mention it again! Unless a patron reads that article and subsequently starts using the service, future newsletters are a wasted opportunity! In some cases, a patron may have read the article and may simply not be impressed enough with the service to try it. Obviously, you don't want to reprint the same copy time after time—so how then to approach newsletter advertising?

Keeping It Fresh

Rather than recycle content, look for new approaches to selling a digital collection. Digital collections are rarely static. When changes (for the better) occur, they represent an opportunity to reintroduce your public to the collection. Some such instances include the following:

New Additions to a Collection

Most digital services represent a series of license agreements among a library, an aggregator (the digital service), and a copyright holder (publisher, film studio, etc.). When a new agreement is forged between a copyright holder and the aggregator, the library's access to new materials may be greatly improved. In the case of an eBook service, you may gain access to a new publisher or author. In the case of a publisher, they may have a focus on a genre, which could suddenly boost this area of your collection overall. Gaining access to a popular author can also strengthen an area of a collection if they similarly focus on the genre, as well as adding new incentive to using the collection. Your other digital media types may also gain a new artist, label, or movie studio. Keep note of such changes!

When a major addition occurs, consider it a qualifying event for a newsletter mention. A headline like "Stephen King added to Our eBook Collection" or "Stream AMC TV Shows" can attract new users or win back those who stopped using the service. This second category is important to note. Patrons tend to have a static view of your library's digital collections. They may try it once and then decide if they like it or not. Rarely do they revisit it time and again looking for improvements. It is up to you to communicate these to them!

Support for Additional Devices

One of the frustrations that come with a digital collection is that compatibility issues can exclude some portion of your patrons. A service may work fine on iOS devices, but not on a Kindle Fire. It may work on Android, but only certain versions of the operating system. Over time, a service may add to its list of compatible devices. This is hugely important! It is the digital equivalent of your library adding to its service area! As each new operating system or device is added, you have a new pool of users—if you can attract them.

These compatibility events are hugely important. Give them the emphasis in the newsletter they deserve. You can also pair this news with associated classes on either the service or the device itself. The two are inextricable. You are telling your patron, "Here's a service you can use, and here's a class on how you can use it."

Other Improvements to a Service

Perhaps a collection has a new and improved layout that makes it easier to navigate. It may have added an app where before there wasn't one. Your library may have increased the checkout limit or loan period or added the ability to request a purchase or place an item on hold. As many of these features are in response to patron feedback, communicating them to your public may win new users and win back old ones who became disenchanted with a collection.

Anniversaries, Holidays

Announcing the anniversary of a collection is an easy way to get a newsletter mention. Pairing a mention with some historical circulation data can be an engaging way of talking about a service. No one wants to be left out! Demonstrating a large user base or total checkouts can indicate that a collection is special and worth trying out.

The holiday season is an excellent time to publish a newsletter article detailing any and all of your digital collections. In the period following Thanksgiving through early January, a large number of gadgets are purchased and gifted. Putting an article in your newsletter showcasing your digital collections and the assistance you offer during this period can be invaluable. In some cases, it will inform the purchasing decisions of your patrons. For example, they may wish to purchase a device for a loved one, which is compatible with a source of free digital content, such as eBooks or streaming movies. For patrons who have received a new tablet or other device, reading about these services post-holiday can get them interested in using them!

Print Ads

Print ads placed in newspapers can use much of the same content as your newsletter copy. In particular, the holiday options we just examined are perfect in this instance. On holidays, you are able to hit on all digital services you offer. The article you will write is topical and timely. Packaging the collection along with your help services is a nice way to showcase the new library. When placing ads, however, be aware of the paper's audience. Advertising services to people outside your district serves no one! Ideally, the paper you choose will cover your service area both in the region covered and its subscriber base. Local papers can be a source of fairly inexpensive advertising targeting your patrons.

Labeling and Processing Standard Media

Earlier, we discussed the impracticality of labeling individual items versus targeting promotions to your holds. This remains true, with two exceptions: when an individual collection is small and if you are not the one doing the work! Let's look at the first scenario.

Consider your magazine collection. Generally, while you may offer a breadth of titles, it is a fairly manageable collection. We examined the placement of a poster in a specific area housing this material, but it is an easy enough task to process the magazines themselves. If you library offers digital magazines, simply add a label that reads "also available online," directing your patrons to its digital twin. This job may be made even easier depending on your circulation rules. For example, if the newest copy doesn't circulate, you can place it in a protective cover and simply label the cover itself. In this scenario, you'd only need to label one item per individual subscription and rotate new copies into the cover as necessary!

Outsource It!

If you are currently outsourcing the tech processing of library materials, examine the possibility of adding some additional labeling, pointing your patrons in the direction of your digital collection. Vendors such as Midwest Tapes, which offer both access to digital movies, music, audiobooks, and other materials through their Hoopla service and processing of traditional audiovisual materials, may be able to market one with the other. Even if the company processing your materials does not offer digital content, it is worth investigating the cost and feasibility of adding a promotional label on items. If it can be done at a reasonable cost, both in terms of money and staff time, you may find it a worthwhile investment. In Figure 3.2, we see an example of a pre-processed insert calling attention to a digital collection.

All these approaches can be undertaken using tried and true methods library staff members are generally familiar with. Many represent low-tech

Figure 3.2 An example of using an insert in physical media to draw attention to a digital collection. Photo by Sara Roye.

and, consequently, low-cost approaches. In addition to the focus on print, there are other well-established methods of marketing library materials and services to our public. I'm talking, of course, about social media.

SOCIAL MEDIA MARKETING

Almost any discussion on marketing must include a social media approach. Social media marketing is inexpensive, powerful, and immediate. Done correctly, it can be used to greatly boost awareness and ultimately use of your library's digital collection. Social media has grown substantially to include services such as Facebook, Twitter, YouTube, Pinterest, and Instagram. With so many options, how should your library approach social media marketing?

Do at Least One Thing Well

With the sheer number of social media sites, you may be tempted to use a kitchen sink approach. Inevitably, this results in quantity over quality. A well-planned, effective social media marketing campaign requires time and attention. If your library has already invested in one or several social media platforms, consider using one or two of them to start off, with their popularity with your patrons weighing heavily in your decision.

Despite the many social media sites out there, Facebook continues to have the largest number of active users. It is suggested that you use a Facebook account as a primary tool, with other social media options acting as a supplementary approach. Once you build an effective campaign, you can of course expand on it by using additional platforms. If you are just starting out, you will likely need to grow your audience before it can be used as an effective tool. I'll discuss how you can do that shortly.

Develop a Social Media Policy

A social media policy acts as a set of guidelines governing both staff and patron behavior. The Harrison Public Library has a good example of a social media policy. In it, they first defined social media before issuing a simple, concise statement on how the library will use it and the acceptable behavior by the public (Harrison Public Library 2015). More importantly, this information is readily available on their website. It is also recommended that you place this policy on your social media site itself. Generally, this can be done under your "about" section or, in the case of Facebook, posted as a note.

Having a social media policy will go a long way toward instilling confidence in the staff responsible for maintaining these sites. With a list of guidelines, they can enforce rules fairly and consistently. With regards your patrons, they will be able to see what constitutes acceptable behavior and the intended purpose of your social media site. In the absence of a policy, one staff member's understanding of acceptable behavior may vary from another's. Rules will be enforced inconsistently, resulting in some patrons feeling victimized. Ideally, you want to encourage an open forum of ideas, at least as they pertain to the library and library-related content.

Assign Roles to Staff

Maintaining a social media site can be a time-consuming exercise. You will need to decide who is responsible for the overall service itself. This person will have full account control, with the ability to add or delete users and, in some cases, assign these users privileges. Other responsibilities will include developing and posting content, running promotions, and potentially purchasing advertisements. Finally, at least one person will need to act as a moderator on your social media sites.

Deciding on Content

What types of content can you use to promote your digital collection on social media? Depending on your social media platform, you will need to vary your approach. Let's first look at some broad rules before examining specific social media sites.

Selling the Content Itself

In any collection, content is king! Using social media, you can greatly increase interest in your digital collection by communicating quality to your patrons. In any collection, you'll want to check to see what access you can have to content without being logged in. The more open a collection is, the easier it will be to share content on social media. Make sure that individual titles within a collection can be linked too. This means looking for a permanent URL. A permanent URL refers to a link that is unchanging, rather than one that changes after a period of time or per session. This same advice goes for linking to your digital collection's homepage as well. Many sites will add a string of text onto the main URL. For example, if I was linking to my library's Over-drive eBook collection, I would send patrons to http://downloads.live-brary.com, not http://downloads.live-brary.com/52AC486F-6A30–4222-ACDB-01C50EC604D7/10/50/en/Default.htm. It won't help your patrons if the links you post expire before anyone can investigate them!

Ready-Made Content When you add a new digital collection, you should contact your vendor to see what graphics, if any, they have available as part of a media kit. At the least, you should expect to receive some web graphics for use on your web page or social media sites. Some vendors will go much further, offering you sample social media posts or in-the-box promotions you can take advantage of. High-resolution graphics will pair nicely with many standard posts, adding some flair to a simple sentence or two about a service.

If you have used flyers to publicize your digital collection, you have a ready-made source of graphics. Simply take the original file and convert it to a jpeg, then post it! This works well if your flyers have used a graphical approach. If you've followed a basic format that communicates the "What is it? How does it work? Where can I get it?" format, you can share a fair amount of information quickly.

Think Mobile Increasingly, people are accessing the Internet using a mobile device. Recently, Google announced plans to promote mobile content over standard web pages in their searches (CNET 2015). Ideally, your library has a mobile site. Of course, this is often not the case. All your popular social media platforms have both a mobile site and mobile apps, allowing you to still engage users on their smartphones and tablets. Just because the social media platform you are using may be mobile friendly it doesn't automatically render your content this way. Rather you must ensure your posts are optimized for people using either a standard computer or a mobile device.

Whenever you are using posts comprising text and pictures, you can rest assured that your content will scale correctly on a mobile device. When you are providing links, however, you should test them first to see how well it works for someone not using a computer. Occasionally, this may mean reconsidering content or providing an additional means of access for a mobile user. Let's now look specifically at some social media platforms, starting with Facebook.

Facebook

When crafting a post, it is important to think about the visuals. Photos are among the most engaging content on Facebook and are interacted with at a much greater rate than simple text-only posts. As your library's content appears in your followers' news feed, it competes with other posts for attention. Knowing this, you should utilize a visual approach to help stand out over text-only posts whenever possible, pairing related graphics and photos to information on your services.

Utilizing Photos in a Post

We've discussed several ways to give your digital collection a physical presence. Using photos, you can successfully do the reverse! If your library commonly takes photos at programs, these can be a source of content. Remember that you can use device- and service-oriented programs to boost use of your collection. Promoting these programs will in turn promote your digital collection! In a similar vein, if you utilize device lending kiosks or gadget petting zoos, be sure to post about them regularly, including a photo. Recall our one-on-one tech help? With a patron's permission, you can engage in some compelling storytelling, showing your public how you can remove barriers to using the library's digital collection. Personalizing these services with photos of a librarian and student can be incredibly impactful. In the absence of patron permission, you can still personalize this service by featuring a particular staff member in a post.

Using Your Collection for Visuals While photos are a tremendous way to capture interest, they are not our only source of visuals. Consider your collections themselves. Both eBooks and eAudiobooks commonly provide a sample or preview, as may other media types. This is an excellent source of engaging content you can offer to patrons who may not have an account, app, or even a library card. Provide a link to popular sample content, along with a little booktalk. Generally, Facebook will pull an image from the site you're linking to. If not, provide an image of the book jacket (or other media cover) yourself to boost visibility. A sample post might look like the following:

> Love Tom Clancy? You'll find the first chapter of his latest book here, in addition to over 5,000 eBook titles! Need help getting started? Call us at 000–0000 to set up a one-on-one appointment!

A post like this hits several notes. Of course, a first look at a chapter is a good incentive on its own, but that is just a start. By choosing to feature high-interest content, your patrons will recognize the quality of the collection. You've also given the size of the collection, which helps instill the sense that there's more good stuff to be had. Finally, for patrons who are curious, but unsure of how to proceed, you've offered personalized assistance—all that in a relatively short post. This type of post can be adapted to any of your digital collections that offer samples/previews of content.

Liking Vendors' Pages

The vast majority of the vendors that we get digital content from maintain social media pages, particularly Facebook. There, they often use polished strategies for promoting their services. By following these pages, you can monitor activity on your news feed for potential material that you can repost on your own. This might include contests and promotions! Your library may lack the funds to raffle off a tablet, but there is no cost in giving away one of your vendors'! These sites are also a source of news. When a new author, publishing house, label, or other content is added, these sites will frequently tout the good news. You can likewise share it with your patrons!

In addition to contests, many vendors curate timely content. For example, Hoopla, a streaming movie, music, and audiobook service, creates electronic newsletters that are published on their Facebook page. During holidays such as Halloween, Christmas, Hanukkah, and Valentine's Day, they group popular titles together. Following awards shows, such as the Emmys, Grammys, and Kids' Choice Awards, they likewise list winners and nominees that can be found within the collection. These newsletters are also published to the Web. This is great content that you can post on your own Facebook page or, if you have the ability, mimic these approaches and curate your own content!

Paid Advertisements

Paid advertisements on Facebook are a great way to improve the reach and impact of your posts. If your Facebook page lacks many followers, it is also a way to quickly grow the size of your audience. As advertising on Facebook is relatively inexpensive, it can be approached on most budgets. In fact, you can tailor your ads toward paying for results, meaning you need not worry about going over budget or wasting money on a campaign that doesn't perform. While you can learn in depth how advertising on Facebook works at https://www.facebook.com/advertising, here are the basics to creating an ad.

Determine an Objective If your social media page has few followers, you should strongly consider using an advertisement to gain likes for your page. Doing this will allow you to better reach a larger audience with standard unpaid posts going forward. You're probably familiar with the "if a tree falls in a forest" saying. If you post on Facebook and you have no followers to see it, does it make an impact?

If you have a healthy following on Facebook, your focus can instead turn toward promoting either an event or a post. Under most circumstances, you'll promote a post itself. This works well with a general post advertising a digital collection. As mentioned, it should include a graphic. Advertising on Facebook has a character limit, so keep it concise and to the point. As always, a "What is it? How does it work? Where can I find it?" approach works well. You'll want to provide a link that leads the service directly to your web page. This makes the information actionable for your patron. It also helps you to keep to your character limit, as you're sending the patron additional information.

Advertising an event can prove useful if you're running a major promotion of a digital service or services. While you want patrons to attend your standard classes on services and mobile devices, it is impractical to advertise them on an individual basis. Exceptions may be made if this is the first time you're offering the class and are hoping to build momentum for future offerings. A more practical example of advertising an event is if you are running a major pre- or post-holiday push on your collection. As you have likely made a substantial investment in staff time, this sort of event can rise to the level of considering a paid advertisement.

Targeting an Ad Once you've decided on an objective, you must narrow your audience. While it would be great for the world to know what your library offers, that would be an expensive ad campaign to run! Additionally, most libraries limit their services to cardholders and issue cards to people residing in their service area. It doesn't make sense to advertise to people who are unable to use the service you're promoting! Carefully targeting an audience will maximize your expenditure.

Facebook advertising allows for you to develop an incredibly specific target audience. Based on the relatively small size that you'll likely target (as compared with, say, a multinational corporation), you can keep your profile relatively simple. After limiting the location of your audience to your service district, next consider their age. If a digital collection is intended for an adult audience, don't advertise to patrons under 18 years of age. If a collection is intended for younger children, they might at first seem unreachable, as Facebook's terms of use require that you be 13 years of age. However, you can in fact specify that your ad targets people who have identified themselves as a parent. Simple considerations such as these will limit your audience to those most likely to be interested and able to use your collections.

Optimize an Ad When advertising on Facebook, there are different types of engagement. Is your goal to have patrons like a post or click on it? Perhaps it is getting them to RSVP to an event. When you craft an advertisement, you have the ability to prioritize a particular type of engagement.

Determine a Budget Developing a budget can be daunting. What is a sufficient budget? What might the expected cost be? Facebook essentially charges for results, meaning the cost of an ad is an estimate based on how many people your campaign is expected to engage. This number is set in part by how you targeted your audience. You can set either a daily or lifetime limit when you choose a start and end date for your advertisement to run. As you craft a budget, you are likewise told what the expected audience reach will be. Ads can be modified on the fly, so if you feel a budget is too high or too low, you can raise or lower it. An ad campaign can be paused or suspended at any time. You will receive continuous reporting on your ad from Facebook.

Twitter

Twitter is a popular social media platform that presents some very unique challenges to marketing. More so than Facebook, it is used on mobile devices, particularly smartphones. Posts on Twitter are limited to 140 characters, meaning they must be brief yet still engaging enough to draw your patrons in. How can you successfully use this platform to build interest in and use of your library's digital collection?

With 140 characters, you cannot afford to waste words. You have room for a headline, not an article. Essentially, your tweets have many of the same constraints as a Facebook ad (as opposed to a regular Facebook post). Tweets must capture the attention and, in many cases, be made to direct users to further information. A sample tweet might look like the following:

> Want to stream FREE library movies on your computer or mobile device? Learn how here: (URL to library's digital collection).

A post like this offers a nice teaser to a service that may be of interest to your patrons. Additionally, you are directing them to a source of more information, where they may get started using your digital collection. You cannot waste space explaining; this must be done elsewhere. If your library offers online program registration, you can similarly use an engaging tweet to draw in patrons to the registration page for your service- or device-oriented programs.

Using Images

We all know the saying, "A picture is worth a thousand words." When you're limited to 140 characters, being able to convey meaning without words is exceptionally important. Use pictures to enhance posts or to serve in place of words. Don't just tell your patrons about your gadget petting zoo—show them! Just as we provided a link to further information on a digital collection, you can attach an image of a flyer in your tweet, adding visuals and bypassing your character restriction.

Who to Follow

It is a good idea to follow any vendors of your digital collection. Doing so will serve as a source of information and potential content for your own social media page. Retweeting an interesting, well-crafted post can help promote your collections while saving you time. Occasionally, a vendor may run a promotion you can piggyback onto. For example, Overdrive (my library's primary source of eBooks) ran an eBook Day celebration (Overdrive 2014). Participants could compose a tweet using the hashtag eBookDay for a chance to win an eReader or tablet. Participating in trending/popular hashtags can also gain you followers, though not all will necessarily be in your service area.

In addition to vendors, follow your peers! This might be the central library, libraries within your system, or libraries in your area, if you are a stand-alone. If the library you are following has the same digital collection, you can mirror successful strategies they use on Twitter. If a library doesn't use the same vendors as you, it can still be worthwhile to monitor them. Perhaps you'll find that the grass is greener on the other side! With the growth of digital content, you may discover a new service that can be added to your library.

Finally, follow news sources pertaining to digital media. This can help you keep abreast of trends. Digital Trends (@digitaltrends) and Digital Shift (@ShiftTheDigital) are two good sources of information. It often pays to be proactive rather than reactive.

Pinterest

With Twitter and Facebook, we saw how using images can help draw attention to a post. With Pinterest, you have a platform that is almost entirely based on visuals! Happily, in most digital collections, you are chock full of content! I am talking about the cover art for your movies, music, eBooks, and other digital materials!

Pinterest allows you to create boards that act as categories by which to organize content. You then pin links and images on these boards, giving you a highly visual representation of the content you've collected. These simple features work exceptionally well for curating titles into a digital bibliography! When doing this, recall the importance of locating a permanent URL for your digital titles. Simply put, make sure the link you provide is one that does not expire after a period of time, or there won't be much staying power to your bibliographies! Alternatively, you must ensure that you needn't be logged into your digital collection's site in order to view materials.

Once these two items are addressed, you can begin creating boards full of digital content. The possibilities are endless! Consider the materials you commonly organize into bibliographies. During holidays, you can gather holiday-themed movies, eBooks, eAudiobooks, and music into distinct boards. Between Christmas, Hanukkah, Valentine's Day, and Halloween, you have several high interest titles to curate! Next, look at the genres. In some cases, you may wish to see how much overlap there is between any print bibliographies and your collection. This can be an effective way to quickly build a large collection of boards.

Finally, curate content that is timely! For a streaming movie or music service, consider award shows. Grammys, Golden Globes, MTV, and Kids' Choice awards are all opportunities to showcase your most popular content. To maximize the number of titles you can showcase, collect nominees rather than winners. When these nominees are popular artists, it can help demonstrate the quality of a collection. When people are unfamiliar with the movie or album that is nominated, they are often interested in learning more.

In the case of eBooks or eAudiobooks, there can be any number of popular awards that you can use to curate titles. Consider the Bram Stoker, Newbery, Printz, Sibert, National Book Award, Nobel Prize for Literature, National Book Critic's Circle, and Booker, among many others! Using these awards, you can assemble boards of past winners and nominees. Even if you collection does not have all these titles, the sheer volume of titles should allow you to pin a fair number to your boards.

Using Multiple Platforms in Tandem
Using Twitter to Spot Trends

Twitter has been called the pulse of the planet due to its ability to quickly register trends and break news stories. As you are informing your public of your digital collection, why not take advantage of Twitter's reading to inform your marketing efforts? Use Twitter to monitor trends. When you spot one that is shared by your community, consider whether you have digital content that is applicable.

Imagine a popular band is getting back together! Twitter will likely pick this news item up quickly. If your digital collection includes the back catalogue of this band, be sure to make this fact known on your various social media platforms! While this is a hypothetical situation, it should give you food for thought.

Maintaining Multiple Social Media Sites

If you maintain several different social media sites, it may require a lot of time to keep the content coming for them all. Recycling content is an excellent way to get the most out of the time you spend crafting posts. Let's look at some ideas.

Cross-posting Simply put, cross-posting is when you post the same content to multiple social media platforms. This can be done manually, if necessary, but more often than not, you will want to have it done automatically. You can use third-party platforms such as Tweetdeck or Buffer to not only cross-post but also pre-schedule posts, allowing you to plan your marketing ahead of time. It can also allow you to ensure you have continuous posts, rather than the ones that occur only during a staff member's fixed schedule.

Third-party applications aside, both Facebook and Twitter have settings that can authorize one to post to the other (Twitter 2015).

Manually Reposting Timely Content Consider all the content that you can gather on Pinterest. All these virtual bibliographies are sitting there, arranged into various categories, occasionally browsed by your Pinterest followers. Rather than immediately reposting this content on other platforms, would it not make sense to wait until interest in it is at its peak? Repost your romance novel on Pinterest boards around Valentine's Day and your Bram Stoker Award winners around Halloween. These boards on Pinterest serve as a passive promotion year round and can provide a more direct boost on Facebook and Twitter with targeted reposts.

ELECTRONIC NEWSLETTERS

In addition to social media, there is another simple, widely used method of bringing attention to library materials and services electronically. E-mail newsletters or eNewsletters are a way to capitalize on the widespread use and popularity of e-mail among your patrons to deliver news and information on your library and its services. Simply put, an eNewsletter is a form of e-mail marketing that allows you to create highly attractive digital newsletters to people that have signed up to receive them. As an online medium, they are naturally suited for use in promoting your library's digital collection. Constant Contact (2015) and LibraryAware (2015) are two popular vendors that offer affordable options to libraries. By collecting patrons' e-mail addresses either online using a web form or in person, patrons can choose to stay informed on library news generally or on particular topics, if your newsletters are organized in this fashion. When signing up, a patron would select any topics he wishes to stay informed of, the categories of which are created by the library. Each of these categories represents a mailing list that eNewsletters are routed to.

While you must have at least one main mailing list, there are good reasons to maintain a separate one for your library's digital services and collection. For starters, having one specifically for this topic can allow you to go into further detail than you can on a more general eNewsletter. Patrons who have signed up for a specific digital services/collection newsletter demonstrate a particular interest in the topic. A more casual user might find an overabundance on the topic off-putting. What types of information should you share?

For a general eNewsletter, consider mirroring the content we looked at for a standard print newsletter. You'll of course want to announce when a new service has been added. When an existing service changes—adding new materials, features, and other improvements—communicate this to your public. Upcoming device- and service-oriented classes offer engaging content to this group. Basically, focus on communicating the most important developments concerning your digital collection. For newsletters specifically targeting a digital collections/services mailing list, what types of specifics can you delve into?

Try treating a narrower eNewsletter as a user group focused on use of your digital collection. You can outline tips and tricks to use a service. For example, if a collection allows for both the download and streaming of media, outline the advantages of each. If you notice common problems pertaining to a service, is there a simple remedy that you can communicate to this audience? If a feature of your digital collection is available to specific devices, it can be difficult to share this with a more general audience. It can, however, find a home in this narrower focus.

eNewsletters, particularly LibraryAware, have long been used to feature new and timely library materials, such as books, DVDs, and CDs. You can easily use them to promote new titles in a digital collection of any type. Depending on the size and composition of your collection, you can mix media or feature specific types, such as eBooks, music downloads, and so forth. Generally, a simple description of a title and a link to it should suffice. As new materials are continuously becoming available, you have an excellent source of content that can be sent on a regular basis.

With the certainty that your patrons are online when they are accessing these newsletters, you must structure your newsletters to take advantage of this. Just as it was outlined in the section on social media, use permanent URLs to directly link to titles and online program registration for complementary services. When following the user group model, consider using video tutorials provided by your vendors or created in-house. When a service has an available app, direct patrons to the appropriate app store. Android users should be sent to Google Play and iOS users to Apple's App Store. The easier you make it for a patron to transition from reading about a collection or service to acting on it, the more likely this is to happen.

IN CONCLUSION

With some minor adjustments, many marketing techniques already familiar to the library staff can be used in support of your digital collection. The creation of print materials such as newsletters, flyers, and posters is an established workflow that can immediately be put to use. In a similar fashion, you can easily leverage your existing social media presence to run successful promotions. In the next chapter, we will look at approaches that may lie outside your comfort zone. These device-centered approaches are powerful tools for advancing the awareness and the use of your library's digital collection.

Chapter 4

Device-Centered Marketing

Previously, we looked at ways to use traditional marketing approaches to promote a library's digital media collection. While this allows you several avenues by which to deliver information to your patrons, it is not and should not be the only way. A library's digital collection is steeped in technology. Your patrons will be consuming this library media on laptops, computers, and a slew of mobile devices. You should likewise integrate technology into your marketing approach. This chapter will look at a series of ways to do just that.

PHYSICAL REPRESENTATIONS OF DIGITAL MEDIA

A library might have an enormous collection of digital media. At the same time, a patron could walk through your entire building, through every stack in every department, and never encounter a single sign of it. Posters and flyers are a great start to marketing a digital collection, but there's more you can do to create a physical presence within your building tied to these services.

Digital Book Displays

To help boost circulation or showcase individual collections, your library may construct displays with your print books or audiovisual content. Similarly, there are ways to do either a stand-alone digital kiosk or a hybrid that integrates your digital collection into a more classic display of library materials. Let's start with the hybrid approach.

In this sample hybrid approach, let's market an eBook collection. In this instance, you would display your print materials as usual, gathering a number of new releases or books grouped thematically. When choosing these items, you should check them against your catalog of digital content. Where there is a corresponding digital copy, indicate it in your display. This can be as simple as adding a bookmark in a copy, stating "also available as an eBook." In many book displays, you may provide a bibliography. Why not incorporate the digital into it? Adding an asterisk for items also available as digital content or separately listing these titles is a small matter! Employing QR codes at these displays is also a simple way to take an interested patron directly to your eBook collection. These types of displays are of course adaptable enough to encompass most digital media types.

In a kiosk approach, you should first check to see what promotional software/hardware your vendor offers. In some cases, they may have out-of-the-box floor displays you can use. For example, eBook vendor Overdrive offers a Media Station while 3M offers a Discovery Station serving as interactive displays. The Overdrive Media Station is licensed software that you can place on a touch screen monitor of your choice (although there are optimal specifications). The software itself is an attractive interface, showcasing your digital collection, as seen in Figure 4.1. Depending on the composition of your collection, patrons can view your top eBooks and audiobooks, view samples, and have items sent directly to their mobile device for checkout (Overdrive Media Station 2015). The 3M Discovery Station works similarly, one of the key differences being your hardware and software come bundled together (3M Discovery Station 2015). In the case that a vendor does not offer a display option, it may be possible with some ingenuity to create your own. Let's look at some options!

Choosing Hardware

To start, a large monitor is a near necessity. The size of the screen helps draw in patrons from a distance and can also accommodate those with visual impairments.

The simplest option is to utilize an all-in-one touch screen computer. Doing so will cut down greatly on the peripherals. If this is not an option, you will also need to provide a mouse and keyboard. As a kiosk may be displayed in an open area, connecting it to the Internet with an ethernet cable is probably impractical. Instead, either provide a Wi-Fi-enabled device or purchase an inexpensive wireless dongle.

Lock It Down!

When creating a kiosk, you'll need to secure it using software. While failure to secure hardware can lead to the theft of equipment, generally the size of the computer renders that unlikely. Mice and keyboard are difficult to secure, but they tend not to be a high-value target. Unless you have found the need to similarly guard these items on your OPACs, they should be fine as is. In the case of poorly secured software, however, your digital media kiosk can quickly be repurposed by your patrons into a Facebook station! What you need is some lockdown software!

Simply put, lockdown software is a program that can place a computer in kiosk mode or limit what sites, programs, and functions a computer may allow. While Windows 8.1 can set kiosk mode automatically, other operating

Figure 4.1 An Overdrive Media Station displaying the Community Library's eBook collection. Photo by Sara Roye.

systems will require third-party software to achieve this. A simple-to-use, inexpensive option is Inset Secure Lockdown. With your kiosk software, you can lock a particular website on your display, in this case the front page of the service you're advertising, while preventing access to the desktop, settings, or other websites. If your vendor allows customization of the collection's homepage or if you are able to embed widgets into a site, you can curate content to put its best foot forward. You'll want to lead with a collection's strengths—popular titles, artists, and authors.

When you're using a do-it-yourself solution, consider what the patron can actually do on the page you've locked down. Are they only able to browse? Must they log in to sample preview content? If the service is cloud based, then it's possible for them to complete a transaction at the kiosk and have them retrieve their materials on their personal computer, tablet, or other device. Conversely, if a patron isn't able to do much without staff assistance, it may defeat the purpose of having the kiosk at all.

Locating a Kiosk

Your first consideration will, of course, be access to an outlet. Aside from this, consider the nature of the kiosk itself. What is the material type? Placement near its physical twin probably makes sense. If a kiosk is going to regularly require a level of staff assistance, it needs to be near the staff! In the case of video, music, and audiobook services, sound is a requirement. You'll need to ensure that wherever you place it, the level of sound doesn't serve as a disruption to the library's operation.

The Gadget Petting Zoo

Have you ever been to a petting zoo? A petting zoo, unlike a regular zoo, allows you to interact directly with the animals, walking among them, and petting and feeding them. While you could climb into a lion's cage at your traditional zoo, odds are you'd only be able to do it once (although you would at a minimum get to walk among them and feed them). A gadget petting zoo is a similar opportunity for your patrons to get hands-on with mobile technology and accompanying library services.

Why a Gadget Petting Zoo?

Not all your patrons have had personal experience with mobile technology, never mind your digital collection. The cost of these devices can be a barrier to entry for many. Patrons on the fence about getting a device might want to reassure themselves that a tablet, eReader, or other device is right for them. Similarly, they may wish to ensure that their library is a source of free, high-quality digital media. A gadget petting zoo can help remove these reservations and create new users of your digital collection.

Setting Up a Gadget Petting Zoo
Choosing Devices

You'll want to focus on popular devices. Your second consideration will be the operating system and compatibility with library digital collections. Oftentimes, simply replicating the devices you trained the staff on will be adequate. You did, after all, choose these devices based on the factors above!

Consider also that a petting zoo will require a level of staff interaction. Staff should be comfortable with the devices contained here or else they won't be able to assist your public!

Choosing Services

Many early petting zoos began as a collection of eReaders. At the outset, library digital media was largely confined to eBooks and device compatibility was limited. Quickly, our access to digital media grew to include not just eBooks, but also movies, music, audiobooks, and magazines! While access to all this media is a great thing, it has also added a level of complexity to creating and maintaining a petting zoo. You must decide whether your petting zoo will showcase the following:

No Services Wait! No services? Not all petting zoos need to show the library's collection. Perhaps your aim is to simply expose your patrons to current technologies. Having a set of up-to-date, popular devices affords your community an opportunity to get hands-on with tablets, eReaders, and other devices without having to purchase them themselves. While this same opportunity may exist at a retail store, your library may hold advantages over them.

Your library may be located geographically closer to your patrons. Even if distance isn't a factor, not everyone wants to hear a sales pitch! A petting zoo at a local library can provide a patron with a friendly, relaxed environment that stands in contrast to retail. At the library, a patron can be assured you're not looking to turn a profit when demonstrating a device. It should be noted that even if you're not loading services onto each device, it's a small matter to simply address compatibility when staff members interact either with a patron or with signage.

Showcasing One Service on Multiple Devices In this scenario, you would simply choose to focus on one of the library's digital collections (if there are multiple) and have the service placed on several different devices. There are several advantages to this approach. The setup of one account on several devices can reduce the setup time the staff will need to spend creating accounts. Depending on the service, you may even be able to use one account across several devices. Cloud functions of a digital collection are often a selling point! On the maintenance side, the need to check accounts and services will be greatly reduced. As the staff will be called to help patrons with the petting zoo, focus on a particular service can act as a boot camp, refreshing skills that can sometimes get rusty with time.

Showcasing One Service per Device Placing a single service on each device allows patrons to experience several different library services, in addition to getting hands-on with the devices themselves. While this may seem like an attractive model, it tends to confuse more than it helps. Unless you engage in some clear signage, you may have the effect of convincing your patrons that your services are confined to a very narrow set of devices. Even if this is not the case, choosing which device to place a service on can feel like steering a patron in a particular direction, rather than allowing him to make an informed decision.

All Services on All Devices In terms of all services, I am of course referring to all compatible services. Streaming video may work fine on a tablet, but it's not something that you can work with on a tablet. This is certainly the most complicated option, but when done correctly it can really act as an excellent showcase for your services.

Choosing a Location

Generally, petting zoos are located in your adult services department. You'll want to locate them in a heavily trafficked area or at least have visible signage directing patrons to it. Staff assistance will commonly be needed, so it should be located in the vicinity of a public service desk. We'll talk about security shortly, but ensure that you have a line of sight from a public service desk to the petting zoo. While you can charge devices in advance, it would be wise to locate them near an electrical outlet. You'll also need a table with enough space to allow for the devices to sit atop, as well as accommodate one patron and one staff member.

Security

Once you've chosen your devices and location, you need to ensure they'll be there tomorrow and many days to come! Securing your petting zoo can be a challenge, both logistically and financially. When you're securing equipment, it is a matter of risk assessment. Some security systems can exceed the cost of the item you're trying to protect. While in some instances this may be justified, more often than not a far less expensive option exists. When securing a device, consider the following:

How Secluded Is Your Petting Zoo? Theft is often a matter of time and opportunity. Do you have line of sight to the equipment? How much staff and patron activity occurs in the area in which it is housed? Does a patron need to pass staff on the way to and from the petting zoo? All these factors act as passive security measures. If a petting zoo is particularly secluded, it may require that you invest in a more robust deterrence. On the other hand, if your zoo is very visible and highly trafficked, you can likely purchase a far simpler security system.

Can the Furniture Be Drilled Into? Some security mounts will require that you bolt them onto a surface. If the furniture you'll be locating your petting zoo can be worked on, you may want to explore this possibility. If this cannot be done, you may need to rely on some less intrusive options. Furniture aside, the floor may also be used to bolt some higher standing mounts in place.

Types of Security Devices

With the information above, we can now make an informed decision on the type of security to invest in. Vendors such as MacLocks offer a variety of models to choose from. Broadly speaking, some common options are as follows:

Enclosures

Enclosures are high-security cases that envelop a device on all or most sides. Oftentimes, they resemble an Otterbox or other heavy-duty phone case. This main enclosure is also connected to a swivel or stand, meaning a device may have the freedom to tilt or pivot. Other models may connect to a firm stand, requiring that they be used/viewed as is. One of your considerations must be how important range of motion is when using the device. You probably would want full freedom of movement if your goal is to allow a patron to try out the device itself. If your petting zoo is oriented to demoing a library digital collection, you may be able to use a more inflexible option. If a service is best viewed in landscape or long ways, however, make sure the enclosure comes fixed this way.

Generally, these enclosures and their necks are secured by screws to a fixed point, such as a tabletop. Additionally, some models are built with a floor stand. As some floor stands can be customized with graphics supplied by the customer, this can be a highly visual approach that combines your petting zoo with its signage.

Advantages of an Enclosure Enclosures are highly secure from both theft and damage. Typically, it would take some intent rather than an accident to break a device within one. With this level of security, you are less apt to have to babysit your petting zoo.

Disadvantages While prices vary, enclosures can cost a fair bit of money. They have a noticeable footprint. You may need to drill into furniture. While some models have a key release, others require that you remove a series of screws before removing a device, meaning the device is more or less fixed where it is.

Tethers

Tethers are steel cables that can be attached to a device on one end and then tied around an anchor point. They are a simple, inexpensive solution to securing devices ranging from laptops to tablets and eReaders. On the end that connects to a device, a cable is commonly affixed with an extremely adhesive tape. On the other side, you may install a metal anchor onto a piece of furniture or simply loop the cable around it and lock it.

Advantages of a Tether Tethers are not only inexpensive but also very versatile. While many enclosures are model specific, most tethers can be affixed to any device. Tethers also allow for a full range of motion for patrons using the gadgets in your petting zoo. Your anchor is removed with a key, allowing you to easily move your devices when you wish.

Disadvantages As tethers are light touch security wise, they are easily thwarted by a determined thief. Tethers can be cut by common tools or popped off from the device side with enough force. As the cable is typically attached to the back of a device, you'll likely be unable to put a protective case on your gadgets other than a screen cover.

Securing It with Software

With the tethers and enclosures we discussed, combined with some passive measures, you have protected your devices against theft. We must now turn our attention to securing your device against tampering through software. In a gadget petting zoo, you're asking patrons to pick up a device they may not be familiar with and play around. Obviously, this can lead to some interesting results. If a device is not effectively protected through software, they may become junked up with improper or unusual setting and unwanted apps. To avoid this situation, you need to take advantage of the protections within a device's operating system and/or explore third-party services.

Operating System Solutions Within every device is a series of protections, the most basic of which is a username and password. While you want your patrons to be able to experiment with your devices, this shouldn't come at the expense of keeping them in working order! Restricting the username and password to the staff will prevent unwanted app installs or other purchases. In addition to managing purchases/installs, password protection can further be used to place broader restrictions.

Take an iPad, for example. Within the device settings is the ability to set restrictions. Commonly, you would use them to disable the app store and the ability to delete existing apps. Additionally, the adding of a pin feature can prevent others from tampering with restrictions. For a more managed, less open petting zoo, the ability to access the Web can be removed. Going further, by using the guided access feature, you can even lock a specific app in place!

In a similar fashion, Android tablets allow for the placing of restrictions. You would, of course, require a password to install any app. In addition, consider creating a restricted profile. A restricted profile is much like adding an additional user login on a computer. This new user will have whatever level of access you allow. Using a series of On/Off toggles, you will customize this account. This restricted profile will serve as the patron account associated with your petting zoo.

Android and iOS devices have GPS as a built-in feature, which can serve as another security layer. By enabling iCloud on an Apple product, you can add the "Find my iPad" feature. This feature allows you to utilize the GPS coordinates to locate a lost or misplaced device. In practice, you would enable iCloud during the setup or at a later date within settings. If you needed to locate your device, you would have to sign into your iTunes account on iCloud.com using a computer. At this point, the device would ping its location on a map, if it's able to. It also has the ability to wipe a device, if sensitive information (such as a credit card) is on it. In the case of Android, Google maintains an Android device manager system, with comparable features to "Find my iPad." In the event of a lost device, a user would sign into their Google account at https://www.google.com/android/devicemanager.

To be clear, the location-based security features are simply an added layer of protection and should not be relied on primarily. While effective for lost devices, they can be easily thwarted by a determined thief. In order to ping its location, a device needs to be turned on. Simply turning off a tablet will prevent it from pinging its location. While turning it back on will enable it to be located, a thief will generally have a factory reset performed on a device, rendering it impossible to locate.

Managing a Petting Zoo

You've determined the purpose of your petting zoo, its location, the devices within, and how to secure them. You must now create a staff procedure. Staff will need to know how the petting zoo will operate and what their responsibilities with it are. Some common questions you will need to answer include the following:

What Is the Opening/Closing Procedure? When the library opens and closes, there should be a procedure involving your petting zoo. Much of this depends on the devices themselves and the tethers you've chosen. For example, simple-to-unlock tethers will allow you to remove and reattach devices at the start and end of each day. Who is responsible for putting these devices out and then putting them away? Where are they stored? For security, devices that are removed should be placed in a locked safe, desk, and so forth with limited access. Whether your petting zoo's devices are a permanent fixture or not, there's still more to be done.

Make Sure They're Charged Each morning, devices need to be checked to ensure they are fully charged. At the end of the day, devices should be connected to a charger. Chargers are among the more common peripherals that can fail you, particularly in locked enclosures. An attached charger to a device that is bent, tilted, and pivoted can see a great deal of wear and tear. If this is a common occurrence, you may consider purchasing some inexpensive replacement chargers. You can also consider charging overnight or, depending on use, periodically through the day. This will allow you to disconnect your charger from the device during operation, preventing wear to the wire.

Make Sure the Devices Are in Working Order When you power on a device, ensure that it boots correctly. If instead, you encounter problems during start-up, make a note of it and bring it to the attention of the person responsible for the equipment (if this is not you). Problems aside, you may also receive notice of an update to the operating system or be given an opportunity to back up the device. Finally, if you are using a restricted profile, be sure to enable it at this time. When you go to power off or put away devices at the end of the night, you should similarly check that they're functioning.

Make Sure Your Security Fixtures Aren't Damaged Once you have your fully charged devices and have made sure they're good for use with your public, you'll need to check your security fixtures. Check for damage, intentional or otherwise. Commonly, this can mean fraying of security cables or loose screws on mounts. If an enclosure seems loose, it may need some maintenance before it can be used.

Running a Gadget Petting Zoo

Once your petting zoo is out and available to your public, who is responsible for its operation? Ideally, your patrons are going to feel free to play with the devices and, in some cases, the associated library services. They may also have questions for the staff. Who will answer them? The training model I outlined should mean that your frontline staff members are familiar with these devices. That being said, if a staff member spent 20 minutes with the patron and away from the reference desk, would that prove difficult to handle? If so, consider making it a backup responsibility. Namely, when the staff has off-desk hours, this can also be considered as on call for the gadget petting zoo.

Maintenance While the successful operation of your petting zoo is a collective responsibility, there needs to be at least one staff member acting as the point person. This person will need to keep the station in overall working order. They will manage the accounts governing all devices. That means not just the creation of the accounts and passwords, but their safekeeping as well. This staff member can provide a backup e-mail account to ensure a forgotten password or unauthorized changes to an account don't become an issue.

With the account credentials in hand, this staff member will be responsible for installing apps as the library adds services or in response to patron requests. If a device in your petting zoo becomes, to use a technical term, messed up with unwanted changes or poor operation, they can restore it from a backup. This account access will also grant the staff member the ability to track a missing device. As updates to a device's operating system become available, responsible staff can install them and ensure they haven't altered your settings in a way that needs to be addressed.

Devices should be cleaned regularly. While touch screen devices provide a tactile experience, they also collect grime readily. Let's keep your display pieces looking like something you'd want to touch! Ensure the cleaning solutions you are using are safe for use with electronics. Screen covers are inexpensive and can be replaced from time to time.

Your opening procedure should involve checking security equipment in the petting zoo for damage, but this doesn't exclude someone from taking a more proactive approach. This means occasionally testing the equipment for weakness, as well as closer inspections. This person will respond to issues reported by the staff or those that they themselves discover by making sure the damaged equipment is repaired or replaced.

Even if your devices are perfectly secured, kept up to date, and in working order, there will come a time when they'll need to be replaced. A gadget petting zoo needs to be reflective of, if not the newest mobile technologies available, at least the contemporary ones. If a new operating system comes out and your device is unable to support it, this can be a sign that it's time for replacement. If newer generations of a device have a substantially better features list, you should also consider moving on. This outmoded device may still be used for staff training—particularly if it can support the current operating system.

Device Lending or Try Before You Buy

We've seen how you can provide your patrons with the opportunity to get hands-on with mobile technology through a gadget petting zoo. While this is a valuable service to offer your public, it does have limitations. By anchoring an eReader or tablet to a piece of furniture, you are essentially rendering a mobile device immobile! The patron experience is limited to a brief period of time in and in a library setting only. There are other options that allow a more open experience that you can offer your public. A prime example is a device lending service.

Simply put, device lending is the circulation of library tablets or eReaders. These devices are catalogued and lent for a set period of time to library cardholders. These loans may be short term or long term. The devices may or may not contain curated content. With so many options, how do you decide on a service model?

Choosing Devices

As always, choose devices that are compatible with library digital collections. Consider your budget. This will inform both the type and quantity of devices you lend. eReaders are generally inexpensive, but of course, they are mostly used for reading only. iPads are extremely popular and widely compatible with most library services, but they can carry quite a price tag. Higher-end Android tablets, on the other hand, are similarly compatible with many library digital collections and are usually less expensive than iPads. They can be less user friendly and may lack the same name recognition as an iPad.

Choose a Setup

Ultimately, getting patrons comfortable with mobile technologies is a boon to your digital collection. Patrons that try a library-owned mobile device may decide to purchase one of their own. They may then use their own tablet, eReader, and so forth to check out library materials. The question is whether you want to curate apps and services on your lent devices or turn the keys over to the patron to set up the device how he wants. Let's look at the two models:

Do as You Please This model allows your patron the greatest flexibility when using a device. It can be a scary thought to lend a blank slate device with no account information, apps, or security software on them, but it can actually result in far less maintenance. At the Mastics-Moriches-Shirley Community Library (MMSCL), we have employed this method successfully using Nexus 7 Android tablets.

Simply put, our devices are factory reset, meaning they require the basic setup a brand-new device would need in order to be used. Enclosed with the tablet is a getting started guide, which walks the patron through the setup of the Nexus, as well as how to get staff assistance. We also bundle information on compatible library digital services. As it is an extended loan, it comes with a charger as well.

When a patron checks out a device, she simply sets it up using a Google account, which, if she doesn't have one, can be made for free at that time. At this point, they have full control over the device, meaning they can customize it to their taste, by looking at what apps are on it. They can set it to send and receive their e-mail. For the three-week period we loan it, it's essentially theirs. Once the lending period is up, we simply perform a factory reset on the device, wiping away all the content and information on it. This removes all privacy concerns for the patron and clears it for use for another borrower. Directions for performing such a factory reset or otherwise restoring from a backup are widely available on the Web.

What Would You Need for This Service Model? Generally, this approach works best with tablets. The wide range of things you can do with a tablet versus an eReader makes the payout for taking off restrictions far greater. Once you've chosen a device, you'll need to purchase a representative amount. Under the do-as-you-please model, you'll need to circulate devices on an extended loan rather than in-house use. It is simply impractical for a patron to go through the process of setting up a device only to have it for a few short hours. Understand that initially there will likely be a great demand for devices, but as they age, interest will wane. With these considerations, it is best to start conservatively, note your holds list or circulation numbers over time, and act accordingly.

In addition to the devices themselves, you should strongly consider a protective case. At a bare minimum, have a screen cover on the devices. When lending Nexus tablets at the Community Library, we use Otterboxes (2015), which are heavy-duty protective cases that enclose a device completely. They are a combination of hard case and soft rubber, which can protect devices against most drops. You will need to provide a charger. Without one, you'll be limiting the patron to the battery life! A simple setup guide should be included, with instructions on where to get additional staff assistance. As you are using this service in part to help boost the circulation of your digital collection, be sure to provide literature on these services! I'll outline a user agreement shortly.

What Are the Advantages of This Approach? Freedom is a beautiful thing! A patron with a clean slate device is able to most accurately measure whether or not it's for him. While using library media is important to us, it is likely not the only motivating factor for a patron considering a purchase. Rather, they'll want to download apps, use the Web freely, use social media, and so forth. By customizing it to their liking, a borrower will make an informed decision. As I'll demonstrate shortly, lending devices with a library profile is time-consuming. You'll need to curate apps and potentially use third-party software to lockdown a device. Even then, privacy concerns may lead you to restore a device from backup anyways!

What Are the Disadvantages of This Approach? A do-as-you-please model requires a long-term loan, which in turn may necessitate that you buy more devices. Even with an extended loan, not all patrons will want to go through the device setup and account creation. When a device is returned, the factory reset option is time-consuming and not all staff will be comfortable doing it.

Lending Curated Devices

In this model, the devices you will lend will already have an account on them. With an account in place, the library will then add apps and other digital content, as well as place restrictions on certain functions. Depending on the level of control you wish to exert, you may also use third-party software to lock a particular set of apps in place. As the device is set for immediate use, you can choose to either do a same-day loan, where a patron can check out and use the device in-house only, or do an extended loan as we outlined in the do-as-you-please model.

What Do You Need for This Model? You will, of course, need the devices you'll lend. Generally, this will be either an eReader or a tablet. Once you decide on the devices, you should decide on the content. In the case of tablets, you will choose some popular apps to place on the device, since your patrons will be unable to download them themselves. This should also include the apps that go with your associated library collections. With an eReader, digital rights management (DRM) will probably require you to purchase and download eBooks in advance. You can save money by placing the same title on multiple devices. Adobe Digital Editions (used to manage the epub format of eBooks) allows for six copies of the same title on both computers and mobile devices (Adobe Digital Editions 2015). Anytime you are making a purchase, you should use a gift card in place of a library credit card. This will limit your liability to the face value of a gift card should an account be compromised.

Since patrons are unable to add media or apps themselves, you need to have a process in place where patrons can make requests. Much like libraries develop collection development policies, you need to have a set of rules governing how content is added to the devices you lend. You may wish to add a print copy of this policy along with a patron request form. When a patron wishes an addition to be made, she simply fills out the form, which is routed to the person responsible for managing the devices. If the app or other media meets the standards of your policy, this person may then install the app on your devices.

Locking Down a Device Curating content isn't practical if patrons can easily erase it all! You also don't want patrons purchasing apps and digital media on the library's account! How can you practically lockdown lent devices? First and foremost are the password protections and subsequent restrictions you place on a device. Using these, you can largely prevent unwanted installations and deletions, as well as prevent the most disruptive settings changes or at least easily undo them by restoring from a backup. For further peace of mind, however, there is also third-party software that you can use to secure a lent device.

Vendors such as 42 Gears Mobility Systems offer mobile device management software (42 Gears Mobility Systems 2015). Device management software is a powerful tool that can allow you to lock a device to a specific set of allowed apps. Furthermore, it can block unwanted peripherals (preventing the use of Bluetooth), prevent any changes to settings, rather than just some, and allow you to manage these profiles remotely. In general, you purchase a set number of licenses (one per device) and then install a proprietary app. Once you verify your account in the app, you can begin customizing your device with the settings and permissions you want.

Advantages of This Approach By curating content, you can create a consistent experience for your patrons. Preinstalling library digital media apps will allow you to more easily showcase your collections to borrowers. While most devices will allow you to password protect the installation and deletion of apps, device management software is a near requirement for preventing changes to settings. A curated device is one that requires no setup, meaning a short-term loan is a viable option.

Disadvantages of This Approach Curating content is no easy task. Developing the collection development policy regarding your devices is a serious matter and should probably be undertaken by a committee. Depending on the level of satisfaction with the apps you have on your devices, you may find that you are responding to numerous patron requests. The nature of these requests is ultimately reactive, as you seek to improve content via patron feedback. Mobile device management software represents an additional cost. Loaning devices with or without this software will likely require that you restore devices from a backup when they are returned so that you can remove patron information from your apps (such as cardholder information on library digital services).

Requirements for Both Device Lending Models

Regardless of the approach you take, you will need to address the following:
Returning a Device Equipment loans can be expensive! You of course want to ensure they're returned, as well as encourage responsible use by your patrons. A user agreement can go a long way toward achieving both. The key elements of a user agreement are the following:

- ***The terms of the loan:*** What is it being lent? How long is the loan period? What are the late fees if a device isn't returned in time?
- ***What are the patron's responsibilities?*** Does a patron need to return a device charged? It can be difficult to determine if a device is in working order when it comes back with a dead battery. What is the replacement cost of a lost or broken device? Peripherals such as the charger and case should be itemized.
- ***Staff responsibilities:*** When a device is loaned, there should be a process ensuring the device is in working order. It's hardly fair to hold a patron responsible for a device that the library had lent already broken! There should be a field on your user agreement where a staff member signs off that the device was lent in good working order.

Checking Devices Out In the case of a short-term loan, you may be tempted to simply ask for a photo ID. To best encourage responsible use, I strongly suggest you have patrons check the device out on their library card. This will help restrict the service to library cardholders. Additionally, checking out an item removes the need for the staff to hold on to photo IDs, typically a responsibility neither the staff nor the patron is comfortable with. Even with an item checked out, you may wish to use some form of credit card preauthorization.

Much like our user agreement, credit card preauthorization is a method of ensuring responsible use of library-owned equipment. Indeed, the two go hand in hand. Your user agreement outlines the cost associated with a lost or damaged device. A credit card preauthorization is a means of enforcing these rules. It is a drastic measure and should be employed if you are circulating expensive equipment and have previously noted a high rate of theft. An eReader is fairly affordable and may not need one. Tablets, on the other hand, can cost hundreds of dollars. Exceptional measures should only be taken if you feel they are a necessity. Even then, this information should only be taken if your organization is able to properly secure and dispose of it as necessary.

Final Thoughts on Device Lending

Despite its expense, device lending can be a powerful tool in promoting your digital collection. As borrowers build comfort and confidence with mobile technology, some of them may go on to purchase their own devices.

When they do, they will have had the opportunity to familiarize themselves with your digital collection. As far as your digital collection is concerned, it's like signing up new patrons for a library card! Thought of in these terms, the cost may not seem as high.

Remembering Your Children and Teen Patrons

While promoting your digital collection, it is possible to forget about your children and teen patrons! With all the focus on adults, these groups represent an underserved population. By focusing some time and attention on marketing your collection to them, you can expand use and hopefully create lifelong users. Before you can market to these groups, you must first do some background work.

Assess the Age Appropriateness of the Collection

You don't want to put inappropriate content into the hands of minors! One of your first tasks must be to assess the age appropriateness of your collection. In an eBook or eAudiobook collection, you'll want to ensure there are children and young adult authors. In a streaming music collection, check that there are children's artists, or that clean versions of adult albums are available. Likewise, a streaming movie service should have titles rated G, PG, or PG-13 (depending on your audience).

Can You Restrict Access? Just because a collection contains children and young adult content does not make it age appropriate. If adult content sits side by side with juvenile materials or if adult material is easily navigated to, you may not be able to market your collection to this audience. Examine your collection development and materials policy for consistency! If your digital collection is set to work with your integrated library system (ILS), see if it understands patron types. If a vendor can differentiate among juvenile, adult, young adult, and any other card types you are using, then you may be able to have them restrict access by age appropriateness.

Is There a Separate Interface? Some collections may offer a separate gateway for teens and/or children. eBook vendor Overdrive offers an eReading Room for kids or teens (Overdrive 2015). This eReading Room serves as a separate site, allowing you to only display juvenile or young adult content. Additionally, content can be browsed by the reading level, making it more navigable by these patrons. Once you're assured your collection is arranged in a way that allows you to practically market it to your juvenile and young adult patrons, how do you go about doing it?

Adapting Prior Approaches to a Juvenile Audience

Rather than reinvent the wheel, you can adapt many of the same techniques you've used with your adults. A kiosk in your children's department that showcases your library's eBook or streaming movie service can attract a lot of interest. With many teens now owning smartphones, there is a strong likelihood that the interest can quickly turn into personal use. Device lending is another great way to promote your collection to this audience, although it comes with caveats.

With device lending, you have the option of a short-term, in-house loan or a longer lending period. With children and teens, I suggest an in-house loan with curated content for several reasons. In many libraries, checking out equipment is restricted to adults. Even if it isn't, the burden still falls on them. If a tablet is returned broken or not returned at all, who will you be billing? A parent isn't going to be happy if they discover the library lent a tablet costing several hundred dollars to a minor! You can, of course, have an adult sign any agreement or check out a device on the child's or teen's behalf. Even then, if you're hoping to circulate a factory-reset device, it will require account creation. Most companies have a minimum age requirement. Google, for example, requires that you be at least 13 years of age (Google 2015). This may necessitate the parent to not only sign an agreement with the library for a device's use but also check it out on their own card and then create an account with its parent company.

If you instead do some in-house lending, you can easily curate age-appropriate content, including, of course, your library-related apps. Even better, there is free lockdown software just for this purpose! For an easy-to-use, kid-friendly model, try Kids Place for Android/Amazon tablets (Kiddoware 2015). For iOS, their built-in parental controls can be used to effectively manage in-house use (Apple 2015a).

Summer Reading Club Promotion

In many libraries, summer reading club is a large-scale event, drawing in many people of all ages. As the theme is reading, why not use this as an opportunity to promote your eBook and eAudiobook collection? If your library has a reading club website, be sure to provide a link to age-appropriate content. If not, you can still use your reading logs, flyers, or other print materials to direct parents, children, and teens to these collections. Building awareness of your eBook collection is the least you can do in the summer. Perhaps you can consider taking it a step further and incentivize eReading!

Consider a special raffle designed to promote your eBook collection. Patrons who read and report on an eBook title receive a special or additional raffle ticket. When doing this, you'll want to ensure that you're being fair to your public. Not everyone has an eReader, computer, or mobile device. The cost of these items can be a barrier to entry. The library has always served as a great equalizer. There are ways to ensure everyone can participate in this promotion.

If your library lends tablets, then you can provide patrons who don't own their own device a means of accessing your digital collection. If you're looking to build awareness, then you don't necessarily even need a patron to read an eBook. Instead you can direct them to a kiosk or public computer that is displaying the eBook collection. Simply have them name a title that's included in the collection or otherwise demonstrate a basic familiarity to receive a bonus raffle ticket. Doing this can at least spur interest in the collection.

Finally, your prizes themselves can be based around your digital collection. Include tablets and eReaders as prizes. As part of the package, you can create a gift basket with information on your applicable digital services and an appointment for getting started in using them. As patrons tend to check out the prizes in advance of a raffle being drawn, they act as a passive promotion of these services to people other than your winner.

Crashing a Program

Crashing a program is simply making an appearance at a program for the purposes of promoting a digital collection. Obviously, we're not talking about disrupting it! Rather, you can appear before a program begins or at its end to make a short sales pitch. If a program is more open ended, there is the possibility of a sustained presence throughout. What are some approaches you can take?

If your library was showing a movie, this would be a great opportunity to talk up your streaming video service! While you have your projector set up, attach a laptop or tablet to it, navigate to your digital collection, and show a quick clip. Wouldn't that be some coming attraction?! After relaying some basic info to your patrons, you can direct them to where you'll be leaving some flyers, as well as where they can get more help. This is a no-cost, high-impact method. With movie screenings, you often have a sizeable audience; plus the existing program setup can accommodate you without the need for additional preparations.

If you were hoping to promote an eBook or eAudiobook service, you might turn to your book club. Book clubs are composed of some of your most avid readers—turn them to a new source of material! Before or after a discussion, you can tie your digital collection to the program. Show your patrons where they might find the next book in the series (if it is a series), another title by that author, or similar reads. Perhaps the next book you'll be reading in the club is available in your collection! For patrons who must wait for a pool collection of titles, the ability to immediately get the next book can be attractive. You can do this with a projector and laptop or connected device. Often, these book clubs are smaller, more intimate settings. This being the case, a projector may prove unnecessary. Instead, demonstrate with a tablet in hand.

IN CONCLUSION

A device-centric approach is an essential component of the overall marketing of your library's digital collection. While you can achieve much with traditional print and social media marketing, more is needed. By adding devices to the mix, you are helping to remove another wall between learning about a service and using it. The simple introduction within the program of a tablet or computer-based demonstration can jump start use. On a deeper level, kiosks and gadget petting zoos offer hands-on opportunities to try and conceptualize current technology and library digital media. Device lending may extend and personalize this experience. Used in tandem with your traditional marketing approach, you are engaging a broad base of potential users. Still, there is more to do. In the next chapter, we will examine how to bring the library's digital branch to the far corners of your community through engaging in outreach.

Chapter 5

Engaging in Outreach

One of the great advantages of a digital collection is its ability to be accessed by those who are not in your building. This is especially important when distance or mobility prevents these patrons from getting to your library easily. While these folks are a natural fit for these collections, they may not even know that they exist! In this book, we've seen a multipronged approach to marketing. Even so, these patrons may not read your newsletter or follow you on social media, let alone enter your building where they might see print advertisements. In order to bring these patrons to your digital collection, you must bring the library to them. This, of course, means outreach!

Performing outreach with your library's digital collection poses its own set of challenges. In order to achieve the best results, you'll need to carefully plan an approach that works within your unique community. Your library may offer a number of digital collections, as well as programs and services in support of them. Not all of these will apply to every venue and those frequenting it. Evaluating your services and then considering the needs and interests of your intended audience should occur prior to an outreach effort.

IDENTIFYING PARTNERS

Are there other entities you can partner with? By finding organizations to work with, you may expand your reach beyond your own building. Other organizations may attract customers that don't frequent your library. Some common partners that the Community Library works with are as follows:

Schools

Schools should be near the top of your list! Recalling age restrictions, you must ensure the collection you are promoting is age appropriate. The advantages of having an effective partnership with the schools cannot be overstated! Not only do you have the potential to reach the youth of your community, but organizations like the Parent Teacher Association also offer you an opportunity to meet an adult audience. As any parent can attest, schools also send home quite a volume of flyers—wouldn't it be nice to be a part of their distribution list?

Houses of Worship

Houses of worship attract patrons of all ages. Many offer classes and activities both related and unrelated to their respective religion. Cannot a class on library digital services or a basic tablet class be one of them?

Chambers of Commerce

Consider your local chamber(s) of commerce, particularly if a collection has any business applications, for example, staff training. Nonfiction eBooks and video on topics such as common software, customer service, and marketing may be of interest to this group. Even if a collection is more oriented toward entertainment, it can still be a desired commodity. Waiting rooms at doctor's offices, mechanics, and other businesses commonly provide their customers with reading materials and movies. Surely the option to provide free digital content might prove attractive to them!

Public Parks and Beaches

Public parks and beaches can be exceptionally popular when the weather is nice. Conversely, libraries are sometimes considered when the weather is less than ideal. Despite this, it is not uncommon to see people reading at these venues. Devices like the Kindle specifically advertise their glare-free eReader as an outdoor reading option. Often, outdoor reading is summer reading. Shouldn't your library build awareness that you are offering cost-free content, particularly during summer reading programs?

Supermarkets and Big Box Stores

Supermarkets and other large stores benefit from excellent foot traffic. Surely you've encountered the Girl Scout cookie salespeople outside one of these venues? A simple station advertising your digital collection and offering hands-on demonstrations can quickly reach a large number of people who may not be entering your library! If you can be half as successful in moving digital materials to your patrons as the Girl Scouts are at moving their products, you're in for a real boost in circulation!

WHAT DO YOU NEED TO START?

Outreach starts with a staff member's presence, and from there it can be augmented to fit the venue and a library's budget. That means a knowledgeable staff member who can speak clearly and confidently on your library's digital collection. Anyone who has successfully completed your frontline staff training should be capable of assisting patrons, but you'll likely want a little more than that for outreach. For outreach, you're looking for salespeople that can engage customers in conversation, learn their preferences, and then match collections and services to them on an individual basis. Doing this takes true people skills and, more importantly, the ability to convey enthusiasm, which cannot be taught! The staff aside, there are material considerations as well. Let's look at a multitude of items and equipment that can be used to help your outreach efforts before turning to some practical setups. Note that this is an exhaustive list of items you can bring rather than the essentials.

Signage

As you'll be operating outside your library, you'll want to identify your organization and the reason for its presence. If you're doing indoor venues only, you may be able to get away with using a simple sign printed on paper that bears your library's logo. At a minimum, lamination is recommended! As you reuse this sign, however, it is likely you will need to constantly replace it. Vinyl signs are an inexpensive and far more durable solution! Vinyl is weather resistant—a must at outdoor venues! In all cases, it can be moved, folded, and unfolded without causing damage.

Print Materials

Bringing any and all flyers that apply to your digital collections and the programs that reinforce them is a simple way to get information into the hands of your patrons. Depending on the venue, you may choose to display these materials with an acrylic holder, or you may need to anchor them with a paperweight in some outdoor situations!

If your library is offering one-on-one tech appointments, there are materials you can bring to promote them. Business and/or appointment cards are a nice way to turn a brief interaction with a patron into a future sit-down in a more planned setting. You can likewise bring a paper appointment book if your library isn't booking online or cannot access Wi-Fi at your outreach venue.

Wireless HotSpots

While not essential, it can be very difficult to promote a digital collection without access to the Internet. In some outreach venues, you may have an open network or permission to use the organization's access point. In other cases, Wi-Fi may not be available or you will be unable to obtain permission to use the owner's. Luckily, it is possible (and desirable) to bring your own Wi-Fi hotspot!

Cellular companies such as AT&T, Verizon, and others offer portable Wi-Fi hotspots. Essentially, there are small devices that broadcast a secure wireless network. Like any secure network, it requires a password to connect to. Your library (and anyone you choose to give access to) is able to connect to your hotspot with some restrictions. Generally, a wireless hotspot has a limit to the number of devices it can support.

Unless you plan on a substantial presence, a basic hotspot capable of supporting five to ten devices should be sufficient for most outreach efforts. Much like a cell phone, hotspots require a data plan, meaning you will incur a monthly charge and have a limit to how much data you can use. Going over a data plan will mean your library will incur additional charges. While you want to avoid going over your data limit, you also don't want to overpay for more data than is practical.

Consider first what types of functions you are looking to perform. Some activities require more data than others. General web use isn't terribly data intensive. What about using your digital collection? Downloading an eBook uses very little data. Your average eBook is somewhere between one and five megabytes—a drop in the bucket (Safari 2009). Streaming music can use a fair bit of data, about 20 megabytes an hour, while streaming a movie can use closer to 300! While streaming music and movies can be data intensive, your use is even more substantial if you choose to download these media. As a general rule, you should only download over standard Wi-Fi, not over a 3G/4G mobile hotspot! Many data providers offer calculators to help you consider your usage (ATT 2015), in addition to real-time monitoring of actual use.

Mobile Devices

Mobile devices can be used to effectively demonstrate your digital collection to your patrons. As always, you should invest in devices that are popular with your patrons and compatible with your collection! Devices you should consider include your standard eReaders—particularly ones that can access your collection wirelessly (rather than require an additional connected computer or laptop) and the big three tablets: iPad, Kindle Fire, and a high-end Android.

In advance of performing outreach, you'll want to fully charge your devices and pre-install the apps associated with your digital collection. You should also create dummy accounts in several places, starting with library cards. Dummy library cards should be made as stand-ins for the patrons a collection is designed to reach. If a collection offers different access points or access to different contents based on patron type, be sure to have adult, teen, and juvenile cards available for demonstration. In this way, you can demonstrate a kid-friendly collection if a situation calls for it. In addition, you'll want to set up service-specific accounts ahead of time, so you can move straight to demonstrating services rather than getting bogged down in setup.

As always, security is a concern when dealing with mobile devices. Depending on staffing levels and the number of devices you are bringing to a location, you may not need to invest in a mount or tether. Generally, small groups and enclosed spaces are deterrence enough against theft. For example, a meeting at a local chamber of commerce is fairly contained, limited in size, and has the advantage that most everyone knows each other. Contrast that with outreach to a public beach! At this venue, it's wide open and there are a large number of people, some of whom may live outside your service area. In a small venue or if you have the ability to assign a staff member to each device, you should be able to get away without needing additional security. In other cases, you will likely need to invest in one of the options we discussed in Chapter Four.

Furniture

In a public meeting, one would hope you would be given a place to sit and a tabletop to set up on. In the absence of this, you'll need to bring your own tables and chairs. It's best to keep it simple and use easy-to-clean, water-resistant folding tables and chairs. Additionally, this type of furniture is lightweight and easy to move. In more formal settings, a table can always be covered.

If your library has access to a truck or van, you can, of course, go with a more ambitious setup. Later in this chapter, we'll discuss using a bookmobile in support of your digital collection. Bookmobiles aside, it is possible to instead transport an audiovisual lectern or a mobile desk. You could even conceivably bring your gadget petting zoo en masse! In this case, you can avoid the need to purchase additional devices and security hardware.

Giveaways

It's a fact: people love their tchotchkes. With a little bit of branding, it is possible to turn a giveaway into a boost for your digital collection. Printing your library's logo, contact information, and some direction to your digital branch is a great way to get started. When you're choosing your giveaways, you'll want to match them to the venue. Pens and stationery are a simple, inexpensive option for indoor promotions. What is more, you can put a modern twist on a pen by purchasing a dual pen/stylus!

In outdoor venues, many traditional tchotchkes may pose an annoyance. No one wants to carry around a pen at the beach! Instead, think outside the box. Oftentimes a sporty approach works well. During beach outreach at the Community Library, we've had success with inflatable beach balls and small Frisbees imprinted with the library logo and information. These are fun, functional, and effective at getting the word out!

Promotions

Signage can help capture a passerby's attention, but there are other ways to draw them in. While your outreach team should be good salespeople, it can also help to have a little carnival barker in them too! A prize wheel is a colorful way to promote your digital collection. While a prize may sound expensive, there are low-cost and, in some cases, free options that you can award!

Consider your digital collections first. If you offer multiple media types, there is an easy way to fill a prize wheel. In this case, your prizes may be a free eBook, free digital movie rental, free eAudiobook, free eMagazine, and free album stream. These prizes can then be used as a conversation starter about your collection. You can create packages of flyers and getting started guides. A prize might also be "win a free tech appointment." These tech appointments can also be bundled with your other digital media prizes. If budget allows, you can of course offer tchotchkes, right up to a more substantial prize.

Having considered the equipment that may be used in outreach, let's next turn to some setups and models that you may consider. We'll start with the most basic and move our way to some robust options.

THE MEET AND GREET

In this approach, one or more staff members set up a small footprint at a venue and provide information on your digital collection to the public. A simple footprint might consist of a table and chairs for the staff to be seated at, along with your program and service fliers that apply to your digital collection. A sign or banner can help identify the purpose and affiliation of your table. Vinyl signs are relatively inexpensive and can handle wear (including the elements) better than standard paper. If you're in an open rather than formal venue, simply find a high foot traffic area. If it is a public meeting, such as a school orientation or chamber of commerce meeting, you will want to introduce yourself or have a speaker introduce you so you're not just a stranger lurking in the back of a meeting!

While this setup is based around getting information into your patrons' hands, there are ways to make it actionable! This is particularly important in outdoor settings. Many patrons at a park or beach are unlikely to want to take a flyer on the go, although you may have a better success rate as they're leaving. Instead, you may wish to make use of a QR code. Recall that a QR code is simply a two-dimensional barcode that can open a web page (among other things). Rather than have a patron take a flyer, it is certainly easier for them to scan a QR code and take the info to go on their phone or other mobile device. If their plan is to do some eReading, at the venue, you've given them the opportunity to get started using the library's digital collection!

THE PRESENTATION

The presentation is a simple marketing pitch made before an audience at an indoor venue. As such, it requires that the host of the meeting provides you the opportunity to speak, either introducing you or allowing you to introduce yourself. During this introduction, you could formally demonstrate a service using a projector connected to a laptop or device (using an adapter). Much like the open-house style staff training, you'll want to cover the basics: What is it? How does it work? Where can I find it? Why should I use it?

In the case of a live demonstration, Wi-Fi is a necessity. If Internet access is not available, you can bring your own, using a wireless hotspot. Another option is simply to download content in advance. This will allow you to demonstrate specific titles. You can then use a PowerPoint presentation that includes screenshots of the service to give an overall understanding of a service. Unless you're a specific part of the agenda, you'll want to keep your presentation brief. Depending on the forum, you may be able to direct listeners to a table staffed by library employees, containing handouts and other information, when the opportunity presents itself.

LOCATING A DISPLAY OFF-SITE

While thinking of ways to market our collection in-house, we examined book displays of your library's digital content. It is also possible to locate a display at an off-site location! Consider the partnership between the Broward County Library and the Fort Lauderdale Hollywood International Airport. After a discussion with the airport's public information officer, the two sides came to an agreement by which the library placed print and digital signage advertising their eBook collection in the baggage claim areas (Overdrive Blogs 2011). By utilizing a QR code, the library was able to provide a link directly to their digital collection—providing easy access to people on the go! Initially, the Broward County Library offered public domain titles that could be checked out whether or not airport customers had a library card with them, with additional plans to offer cardholder-only content in venues with a higher percentage of locals, such as bus stops.

Agreements like these work best when they are viewed as a net gain for both sides. If your request comes across as an imposition, you may have difficulty. In the case of the Broward County Library and Fort Lauderdale Hollywood International Airport, the venue saw the digital collection as a free amenity they could offer their customers, while the library was able to raise the visibility and use of their collection! Consider this symbiotic relationship when approaching potential partners!

This approach is extremely adaptable and can be done with little maintenance! While airports have the advantage of tremendous foot traffic, by nature they are full of out-of-district residents. Surely you can target a bus or train station for a basic display that integrates a QR code! These venues have well-established rules for purchasing an ad, allowing you to similarly use a sign or poster to target a more local audience. Aside from the station or stops themselves, you could potentially advertise within a train or bus itself. Commuters often read, watch movies, or listen to music and audiobooks; why not offer them free, high-quality library content?!

LOCATING A KIOSK OFF-SITE

The perfect kiosk functions as both a hands-on demonstration and an access point for potential borrowers. While the ideal situation will always involve the staff available to help, it is possible to set up a kiosk that can operate on its own for long periods of time. The San Antonio Public Library is an excellent example of a more substantial footprint, once again taking place at an airport, in this case San Antonio International. Working together, the library system was able to locate two interactive digital library kiosks within the airport, showcasing their collection (MySA 2014). Items can be checked browsed, checked out, and downloaded! What is more, the terminal functions as a mobile device charging station! As it is located within an international airport, a large number of potential customers may lack library cards. The San Antonio Public Library addressed this by working with their vendor to allow the creation of temporary library cards able to access their digital collection!

The kiosk approach may sound daunting, but it needn't be! Rather than customize a kiosk and engage an audience the size of an international airport's customers, think on a smaller scale. Indeed, if you can approach a venue that largely caters to people in your service area, it lessens the need for temporary library cards or limiting a collection's scope to public domain. A community center could fit the bill! There, you could potentially use an out-of-the box solution from your vendor (such as an Overdrive Discovery Station). If cost is a concern, you could use one kiosk on a rotating basis at both your library and an outreach location.

THE ON-SITE TECH APPOINTMENT

One-on-one tech appointments are an excellent way to help high-needs patrons learn to effectively use your library's digital collection, as well as current technology. Without these appointments, some of your patrons might never be able to access this media. If an appointment only takes place inside your library, however, then a percentage of this group will be unable to receive the help they need, due to distance or issues with mobility. Your library may already offer a homebound service, by which materials are delivered directly to a patron's home. Why not deliver some services as well? A digital collection is often the perfect match for these patrons!

Before offering one-on-one tech appointments at a patron's home, there are several important considerations. For starters, you'll likely want to offer them to patrons who meet your definition of homebound or are otherwise unable to make it to your library, unless you have substantial resources to invest in the endeavor! While understanding that these tech appointments are already staff intensive, you may wish to consider sending two staff members rather than one, with both security and liability in mind. Once these issues have been addressed, how might a one-on-one tech appointment conducted in a patron's home look like?

As always, it is important to examine the scope of an appointment. They should in no way offer less than a patron visiting your library, so at the outset they will either be confined to assisting a patron with using your digital service or include general technology help. The nature of these appointments, however, may leave you with a request to do more than you ordinarily would in a library setting. For example, you will find patrons bringing in their mobile device, new in box. Similarly, you may find a patron with a new desktop computer. Does your assistance include this sort of setup?

In a similar vein, a common patron issue in technology appointments conducted at the Community Library stems from a misunderstanding of wireless networks. Occasionally, patrons will mention difficulty in finding their home wireless network, while a reference interview would uncover that they don't own or haven't set up a wireless router! There is an assumption that because they are paying for Internet access, they automatically have available Wi-Fi. Do the library's tech appointments extend to setting up a wireless network? While there are very good reasons to be wary of such an endeavor, there are equally compelling reasons to do so. As information professionals, there are few better ways of empowering a patron than connecting them to the Internet! With the library's digital collection heavily dependent on Internet access, you don't wish to write off a potential digital borrower, when it could be remedied in under an hour!

Even if your service model does not allow setting up a home wireless network, you may still be able to provide referral services. Cable providers commonly offer these services as part of their standard agreement. The library staff can assist in navigating this service. Additionally, the explosion of mobile hotspots may mean a patron has complimentary access to their cable provider's Wi-Fi. Once again, they may need assistance locating their account credentials and properly logging in.

Aside from the wireless network concern, there is another distinction to be made with home visits. While tech help is conducted by appointment, recall that not everyone remembers they've made an appointment. I'm sure we've all experienced a forgotten doctor's visit or *gasp* a library staff meeting! In light of this, it is important that you wear a nametag or other identifying dress. You are entering a patron's home; they are not entering a library where your identity is far more assured! Business cards are a help, but not a replacement for this! Reminder calls the day before can help mitigate these issues, in particular, letting a patron know in advance just who will be helping them. Autoglass repair company Safelite offers a "Technician Profile E-mail" that identifies who they'll be sending, including a photo (Safelite 2015). If an e-mail can bring peace of mind to their customers, could it not do the same for your patrons?

Once you've begun assisting your patron, it should largely resemble a standard tech appointment. That is, of course, unless you choose to offer a different approach to tech appointments. When conducting in-home tech appointments, we considered sending multiple staff members as a safety precaution and a means of limiting liability. If that is an impossibility, then perhaps you can simply choose a venue that is nearer to the patron?

Ideally, the library would choose a public space that gives both parties a degree of security. This might be a recreation center or other municipal building. An agreement should be secured in advance from the appropriate party. In many cases, this will be enough to reach patrons who cannot come to your library on a regular basis. If you can get an agreement with a senior nutrition or recreation center, you may find that these organizations offer transportation to their customers. This does come with some drawbacks, however. Anytime you are using a public venue, you will find yourself dependent on their wireless situation. Once again, it will turn to whether you can secure use of the organization's Wi-Fi or bring your own with a mobile hotspot.

INTEGRATING DEVICE LENDING WITH
A HOMEBOUND PROGRAM

For libraries that offer a homebound program, there exists the possibility of integrating device lending into the service. Within your service area, you may have senior centers, assisted living centers, and other patrons otherwise unable to leave their residence. There are compelling reasons to offer this service to your public. Of course, device lending may allow your homebound patrons the chance to be exposed to new technologies they might not otherwise have experienced. Thinking more basic, however, what is the cost of delivering books, movies, and other library materials? As well you know, the heavier the freight, the greater the expense. Now consider that a standard Kindle Paperwhite eReader can hold approximately 2000 eBooks (Tech Crunch 2014)! A high-end Android tablet or iPad may hold many times that amount, in addition to supporting videos, eMagazines, music, and other media. If we're thinking practically, might it not make sense to simply give (or put on permanent loan) an eReader to your patrons? Such a program would likely work one out of two ways.

DO AS YOU PLEASE

As discussed in Chapter Four, this refers to a factory-reset device, one that arrives to the patron a clean slate, either new or with all its data wiped. A patron then sets up their own personal account in order to use the device to its fullest (downloading media, apps, and other content). In terms of a long-term loan to a homebound patron, your goal is to provide them with a means of accessing library content. In line with this goal, you should at a minimum provide a substantial getting started guide, allowing your patron to navigate your collection. More likely, you will need in-person assistance at the outset.

While the ability for a patron to customize the device to their taste is a real attraction (particularly in a permanent loan situation), there are clear drawbacks. For starters, there is no guarantee a patron will use the device to borrow library media. If your goal is simply to provide technology and entertainment, then this may not present a problem. If it does prove a concern, you may wish to approach it with a curated approach.

CURATED CONTENT

There are several ways to approach a curated device. Taking a cue from Chapter Four, you can pre-install apps and then use a mobile device management software to prevent unwanted additions, deletions, or other changes to the hardware and settings. If your intent is to supply the patrons with library digital media access only, then you'd tailor the account so that the apps associated with your services are available to the exclusion of other ones. Generally, this software is intended for tablets and not eReaders, but there are other ways you can curate content. Additionally, there are ways to remotely deliver digital media directly to your patrons. These models work particularly well with eBooks.

When we think of a library's digital collection, we often think of the media that is lent through a third-party vendor. There are instances where it may make sense for you to purchase eBook titles with the intent of putting them on devices that you loan. These are permanent titles, rather than library copies that expire after a time. These copies then constitute a digital collection that travels with the devices you lend. Using this method, you can place bestsellers on a device for your homebound or other patrons. As some titles are released as eBook exclusives that may not be available on your library's digital platform, you may find this is the only way for you to offer them to your public. Look at the Brentwood Library, in Contra Costa County, California. In 2012, the Brentwood Library launched a pilot program that placed Kindle Touch eReaders preloaded with titles and authors popular among senior citizens in their homebound program (San Jose Mercury News 2012).

If you want to start a similar eBook program, the library would create an account with Amazon, Barnes and Nobles, or another eBook vendor. In the case of an eReader, the devices would be set up using this account. For a tablet, you would install the associated app, such as the Kindle app if you were to purchase titles in Kindle format, and then sign into the account. When you purchase titles, they would then appear on devices sharing this account. Depending on your vendor, ensure that you follow their guidelines for the number of copies you are entitled to with a single purchase.

Prior to loaning a device out, you'll want to take measures to protect the library's financial information. Purchases should be done on a VISA or other gift card to limit your organization's liability. Accounts can be password protected to prevent patron purchases or (depending on the device) they may be removed altogether. Once you've built a library of sufficient size and satisfied any security concerns, these devices can then be lent with preloaded content. A service like this doesn't have to end here.

As new titles are released or you receive patron requests, you can add more content. Many eReaders are 3G/4G enabled, allowing them to update as long as they can find a cellular signal. For tablets, a patron would need either Wi-Fi or your library would need to pay for a data plan, which is inadvisable to say the least. In both these cases, the eBook service's account would need to be active. If it has been disabled as a precaution, or if a connection is unavailable, it is simply a matter of having your patrons return their device for regular updates from the library. Once back at the library, it is a small matter to make necessary changes over your wireless network. Following this, they can be returned to your patron.

WHAT ABOUT OTHER MATERIALS?

Obviously, your homebound patrons aren't only readers. They listen to music and audiobooks, watch movies, and read magazines. Can this service also support these material types? The answer is yes, though not nearly as easily. eBooks enjoy several advantages over other media types for this method of lending. For starters, eReaders can be used in an eBook-only service. eReaders are extremely affordable, commonly costing under $100 per device. Additionally, the ability of many eReaders to receive content over a cellular network allows them to operate effectively even if a patron doesn't have home access to Wi-Fi. The digital rights regarding eBooks make them a more financially viable option, as you can easily place copies of a single purchase on multiple devices.

Despite these difficulties, it is possible to curate other media types for homebound patrons. Rather than purchase content and then load it onto devices as we did with eBooks, see if your library's digital collection of other media types is flexible enough to accommodate this service. As a first consideration, examine whether items in these other collections expire after a time or are considered permanent downloads. As an example, eMagazine service Zinio and music service Freegal both offer models that allow a permanent download of materials. As a result, content can be checked out, downloaded, and used to build a digital library on devices that are then loaned. Using this approach, you can avoid the substantial cost involved in purchasing these materials.

PACKAGING IT WITH A TECH APPOINTMENT

When you lend a device to a patron for the first time, particularly if it is a factory-reset one, it can be helpful to meet with the recipient directly. The ideal tech appointment is one that leaves your patron with the ability to successfully use the device on their own, with little or no troubleshooting on the library's end. More often than not, however, a tech appointment in support of homebound service may require follow-up lessons. A service may change in a way that leaves a patron confused. On the other hand, as your patrons grow more confident in using digital media, they may wish to expand its use. Whereas before they tried reading eBooks, they may now want to use your streaming video service.

Regardless of whether a patron contacts you for a follow-up appointment, you should check in on them from time to time. I've often encountered patrons that seem lost in our stacks, searching for a book. Despite their confusion, they are often loath to approach the reference desk. A simple "are you finding everything that you're looking for?" often leads to them requesting further help and, ultimately, getting their desired materials. Similarly, a call to a patron to see how they're doing navigating your digital content may result in a follow-up appointment or over-the-phone assistance. The result of these interactions is patron satisfaction and, consequently, the continued use of the library's collection.

COLLECTING STATISTICS

While normal digital checkouts are commonly recorded by your vendor and are accessible to the staff, the same is not true of content that is purchased and preloaded onto a device. How then do you measure this collection's use? You would be inflating statistics if you counted each patron that borrows an eReader with a thousand eBooks as a thousand checkouts! On the other hand, a patron with a thousand eBooks at their disposal is likely to read more than one.

A periodic survey may help you gain a sense of the use of this device collection, as well as collect valuable information on the overall health of the program.

BRINGING WIRELESS TO YOUR PATRONS

As we've discovered, a lack of Wi-Fi or home Internet access presents a persistent problem to patrons accessing your digital collection. The New York Public Library has taken a novel approach to bringing the Internet to their patrons. In 2014, they introduced Wi-Fi modems (wireless hotspots) with unlimited 4G data plans that were loaned to patrons for six months at a time (MobileBeacon 2015). After this pilot program of 100 hotspots and a $5,000 budget, they expanded to 10,000 Wi-Fi modems the following year. Under this program, hotspots are lent to patrons who don't have home Internet access and are enrolled in particular library activity, such as an adult education program or after-school program, though they later dropped this enrollment requirement.

It is easy to see how a program like this can be used to increase the reach and use of your library's digital collection. In particular, the aforementioned homebound program could benefit from providing home Internet use to those who lack it. As a large percentage of your homebound population are often senior citizens on fixed incomes, Wi-Fi is often seen as a luxury. A wireless hotspot has the ability to connect them more closely to your library and the world as a whole.

THE FULL-SERVICE CENTER

If your library wished to open a satellite branch for your physical collection, think of what that would entail. You'd need to move innumerable books, magazines, CDs, DVDs, and BluRay. You would require shelving for this material, a circulation desk to check it out and return it, and a security gate to protect materials against theft. Now think of how few of these concerns apply to a digital collection. A physical off-site presence for a digital collection is possible on both a short-term and a long-term basis. With even a basic setup, a full-service center can offer your patrons a large range of services. If you can secure use of an indoor venue and just five feet of table space, you can offer your public the following:

Promotion of the Collection

Do-it-yourself digital signage is inexpensive. A simple outward-facing monitor can display a screensaver or a slide show can assist in advertising. If you wished to save money and real estate, you could also put a monitor used at a workstation on a swivel. When not in use by the staff, this monitor can face away from them and toward your public. A simple screensaver or slide show that promotes the various digital collections and the services and programs that are associated with them can run at this time. Simply taking your existing collection of flyers on these topics and converting them to a jpeg file will provide you with a good base with which to start. If you have access to kiosk software, this can be run on this monitor in place of a slide show, though it would likely limit your ads to one particular service at a time. If you have the luxury of space and a second computer, you can of course run a kiosk as an additional component. A vinyl or other format sign with your library's branding can adorn your space as well.

Tablets and eReaders can be mounted or tethered to your workspace. These devices can function as a gadget petting zoo, with the added bonus of having a staff member immediately available to assist a patron in using them. With a staff member always present, there is less of an incentive to put kiosk software on these devices, unless you anticipate periods of time where they would be left unattended.

Creation of Library Accounts

Bringing library services and materials to patrons means nothing if they are prevented from receiving either due to a lack of a library card. The ability to create library accounts on the spot is a truly powerful way to expand the use of your library's collection. There are two very practical ways to do this; however, both are dependent on third-party vendors.

Granting a Full Library Card

As a first step, you should check with your integrated library system (ILS) to see if they offer a mobile version. In the case of the Community Library, our vendor, Innovative, offers a mobile version of their Sierra platform. This platform has full functionality, allowing us to effectively run a circulation department on the fly, including the ability to grant library cards (Innovative 2015). Assuming your ILS system can be run remotely, you can next proceed to setup.

While it is possible to run a mobile version of your ILS on a tablet, it may not be the most practical way to do this. While touch screen functionality may work well for some forms of navigation, I have often found it limiting when using our ILS system. Bluetooth keyboards may mitigate these issues, but this is an added expense. Additionally, as you continue to layer components onto a process, the more likely one of them is to encounter an issue. Simpler is often better. If you are already using a computer or laptop as a workstation/outward-facing slide show, you can utilize this same device to run your ILS. Aside from simplifying the process, it has the added benefit of saving you space.

When granting cards, libraries overwhelmingly have a residency requirement. As a result, patrons will need to provide proof of address. You cannot reasonably expect a patron to have all the necessary information on his person when encountering the library in an unfamiliar setting. It is therefore important to advertise your presence in advance, particularly if it isn't on a long-term basis.

Granting a Provisional Library Card

If your ILS system does not offer a mobile version, or if your organization isn't comfortable with granting library cards outside its building, there remains another option. A provisional or temporary library card is a way to extend borrowing privileges to a person who might lack the necessary documentation for a full library card. In Suffolk County, New York, consortium libraries are able to direct people to an online service map (Live-Brary 2015b). Once there, the person enters their home address, which then identifies their home library. They are then able to apply for a temporary card by additionally providing a phone number and e-mail address, shown in Figure 5.1.

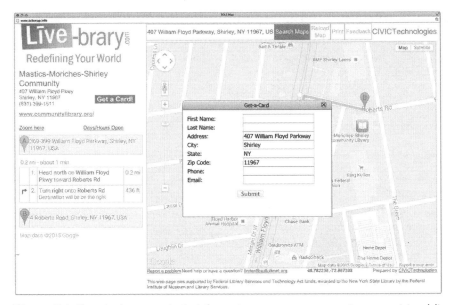

Figure 5.1 By entering some basic information, a patron can receive a provisional library card. This card immediately grants use of the digital collection for 30 days, while directing patrons to their home library where they can become full cardholders. Photo by Sara Roye.

By completing this simple process, the patron is given a library barcode, which can be used to access the library's digital branch. With some exceptions, she gains the use of library databases and digital media collections that require barcode authentication. To gain full borrowing privileges, such as the ability to attend programs or check out physical library materials, the patron must come into the library and complete a traditional sign-up process. Namely, they must provide standard proof of identity and residency. After 30 days, this temporary card expires. While not a perfect solution, it does offer a good middle-of-the-road approach to offering access to those without cards. A temporary card that offers access to your digital collection is a very low-risk proposition. A library eBook or streaming movie is impervious to theft. When the lending period expires, it simply returns to its shelf, even if it adheres to a one-copy-one-checkout model!

By offering your patrons a taste of your digital media, you are incentivizing the library card sign-up process. Consider the difficulty of convincing a patron who finds it difficult to reach your library to do it just so he may sign up for a library card to access a collection he's never tried. Additionally, patrons who are part-time residents of your community may also consider themselves ineligible to use your services. Perhaps you have a seasonal influx of vacationers. If you are located near a college or university, you may likewise see an influx of potential patrons on a regular basis. On a smaller scale, you may have temporary residents staying with family, such as an individual between jobs.

Now imagine you've given a patron the trial use of your collection and they've found it engaging. Surely they'll be more likely to make the inconvenient trip to your library to gain long-term use of this collection! Based on the length of your library card's term, they may only need to make this trip once each year or two. In the case their stay is shorter, this provisional card allows them to use the library's digital collection for information and entertainment and for you to expand its use.

Patron Instruction

With the presence of the staff, mobile devices, an Internet connection, and print resources, your full-service center is well equipped to offer patron instruction. One-on-one appointments can be conducted here, either on a drop-in or by-appointment basis. You'll want to first gage your average traffic at this location to see the practicality of taking drop-ins. As a general rule, drop-ins work much better for patrons attempting to get started using the library's digital collection, as they are usually straightforward and do not require prior research. They can often be resolved much more quickly than device instruction.

Being able to offer your patrons a second location to receive one-on-one instruction, which may be far closer to them than the library itself, can prove advantageous. As you're operating a work station, you'll be offering some level of immediate assistance. Whether you choose to limit the scope more in line with your traditional reference desk is up to you.

Setup

We've examined the range of options you can offer your patrons with a full-service center. Let's now concern ourselves with its setup. If the intent is to operate as a satellite in a public building, then mobility is far less of a concern. A standard desk or table that functions as a workspace will do. Understand that some level of alterations to the desk will need to be made as you attach mobile devices and security mounts to the desk. Unless your hours of operation exactly mirror your hosts', you will need to further secure this equipment. It is suggested that you use tethers or mounts that can be easily undone, with the devices locked in a secure location when not in use. While mounts and tethers may deter theft, with enough time and opportunity one can pry loose an eReader or tablet. In this scenario, a laptop rather than desktop may also be advisable.

If the duration of your full-service center is shorter, or if you intend to move it on a regular basis, a more mobile setup will prove invaluable. At the Community Library, we took a do-it-yourself approach to creating a mobile workstation we dubbed The Digital Desk. In actuality, our desk was an audiovisual lectern that we purchased from Nova Solutions, Inc. (Nova Solutions, Inc. 2015). This desk then underwent a series of in-house modifications.

Initially, we purchased mounts for an iPad, Kindle, Kindle Fire HD, and Nexus 7 Android tablet from Maclocks.com. These mounts were then secured to the front of the desktop with screws. A large 24-inch touch screen monitor was attached to a swivel mount also located on the desktop. On the interior of the lectern, we secured a power strip, wireless hotspot, and computer tower. In the side drawers, we located program handouts and flyers advertising our services within an acrylic holder. Finally, a large sign mounted on the front of the lectern completed the customizations. A picture of this station can be seen in Figure 5.2.

These simple modifications allowed us to create a low-cost full-service station with a high degree of mobility. The desk itself is on iron casters, allowing it to be wheeled where we need it and then locked into place. As it is a lectern, there are cable management features that keep the wires contained, meaning the only visible wire is the cable that runs to the power strip. This power strip contains enough outlets to provide power to all attached devices. A mobile hotspot provides wireless access for up to 10 devices, which covers all staff equipment, plus support for several patron devices. The desk itself requires a key in order to access the inside, making it a practical place to store devices.

Figure 5.2 The Community Library's Digital Desk, featuring secured devices with trial accounts, literature for patrons, and a touch monitor on a swivel. Note the one cord which powers the entire station. Photo by Sara Roye.

On the Digital Desk's computer desktop is a mobile version of our ILS. Also located are several Google forms and documents. There is a spreadsheet and form that serves as an appointment book for one-on-one tech assistance. Here we both take and record the results of scheduled and unscheduled appointments. We separately utilize a form and spreadsheet to record reference transactions at this station. Ultimately, our Digital Desk can be transported in a library-owned van. It is small enough to fit in an elevator and can be moved across a building by a single employee.

OFFERING AN ON-THE-ROAD PROGRAM

An on-the-road program is, simply put, one of your standard device- or service-oriented programs offered at an off-site location. If your library's service area is rather spread out, the ability to offer programs closer to your patrons can help reach new customers. The setup and execution of these programs is covered in Chapter Two. Still, conducting them off-site requires some additional considerations.

As is often the case, access to Wi-Fi is a huge consideration. Classes on both your digital services and patron devices are heavily dependent on a wireless connection. While your venue may allow you to use their network, does the same offer extend to the public? If you cannot secure access for your patrons at the venue, you should instead turn to a mobile wireless device. If your class is to be a regular feature, or if you are using a data-intensive process, like a streaming video, you may wish to invest in an unlimited data plan. You will also want to purchase a device that is capable of supporting your class size. This may mean a mobile hotspot that allows 10 or 20 simultaneously connected devices.

When using a mobile hotspot, the network will be password protected by default. This means you will need to assist any patron who will be connecting to it. As patrons enter your class, you should assist them in signing in, either by giving the wireless password or signing them in. As an alternate option, you may be able to offer a guest login, depending on the device. With a guest login, you can later change the password to guard against unwanted access after a class.

Much like the in-house classes described in Chapter Two, you may wish to make follow-up one-on-one tech help appointments. If your patrons are finding your off-site venue easier to access, it would be advisable to see if you could utilize it at a future date for this purpose. In public venues, this may require permits. While a good rapport with those issuing permits may speed up the process, you will likely need to do some advanced planning, such as setting aside dates in advance to offer these follow-up appointments.

Digital Media Bookmobile

Bookmobiles have long operated as a means of bringing library materials to patrons at an off-site location. Surely there are ways to deliver a library digital media experience using a bookmobile? While a bookmobile can be expensive, there are less costly and, in some cases, free options. Your digital media vendors have an obvious stake in the success of your collection. As a precursor to making any purchases, you should first see what, if anything, they have to offer.

Take the example of library digital media vendor OverDrive. OverDrive offers a DIGITALbookmobile, a 74-foot-long travelling exhibit focused on promoting a library's OverDrive collection (DigitalBookMobile.com 2015). Within this massive space are a series of exhibits, entitled "Digital Catalog, Audiobook Alley, eBook Experience, Gadget Gallery and Video Lounge" (DigitalBookMobile.com 2015, Experience Section). Taken together, they offer quite an experience. Patrons can view getting started videos and be exposed to popular eBook titles and authors. Using a browser-based checkout option called Overdrive Read, these patrons may check out tiles immediately without the required software. Audiobook Alley functions as a listening station, where patrons can experience eAudiobook samples. The Gadget Gallery functions as a substantial gadget petting zoo, offering a hands-on experience that is not just limited to tablets and eReaders. Included are phones and media players, which can be an impractical and expensive addition to the library's collection.

The DIGITALbookmobile likely resembles a wish list for many libraries. The fact that the opportunity exists to request a visit at no cost to your organization makes it a low-risk, high-reward opportunity (DigitalBookMobile. com 2015, Contact Us). When looking at all that the DIGITALbookmobile offers, consider how much of it is achievable with modifications to an existing bookmobile.

If you are looking to add a digital component to your bookmobile, you must, of course, find the room for it. While eBooks, streaming movies, music, and other materials don't take up shelf space, you must provide some sort of hands-on, interactive experience for your public. Computers can be an expensive investment. Their presence usually requires seating and, of course, power. The expense of proper wiring, furniture, and a power source may quickly become untenable. Here's where thinking mobile can aid you.

Mobile device can save you both space and money. Tablets and eReaders can be charged in advance at the library before being taken on the road. eReaders, in particular, can be used for long periods of time before ever needing to recharge. Many eReaders boast a battery life of a month or more, compared with a charging time of just a few hours (TopTenReviews 2015). That you can charge elsewhere eliminates the need for costly wiring within your bookmobile. A tablet, unlike a laptop or computer, can be held in one's hand when using. This can allow you to operate without adding desktop or table space.

A properly functioning digital branch will need to provide a strong wireless signal in order to operate. As bookmobiles are often used in remote, isolated areas, it is not always practical to utilize a mobile hotspot device, as they can struggle to detect a cellular signal. In terms of cost, your standard mobile hotspot should be your preferred option. If you find they cannot adequately perform, you can then turn to a mobile satellite Internet system. Using a satellite dish mounted onto a bookmobile, you can ensure wireless Internet access anywhere in North America. The Chattahoochee Valley Library System in Georgia utilizes such a satellite uplink to offer digital services through their bookmobile, appropriately named The Digital Bookmobile (Chattahoochee Valley Libraries 2015). In their case, this connection is used to offer a plethora of services, including tax assistance, GED preparation, and computer classes.

Consider the breadth of services you can offer your public with wireless access and a handful of mobile devices. A gadget petting zoo can be achieved using simple tethers and/or mounts attached to existing furniture and shelving. It is possible to conduct small group instruction on devices and services, though this may push the limit of your space. Depending on the weather and the reach of your wireless hotspot, you could perhaps offer the class outdoors, in the vicinity of your bookmobile. A few folding chairs could provide seating. More practically, you can offer one-on-one tech help appointments delivered around the scheduled appearance of your bookmobile.

Device lending programs could easily be run out of a bookmobile. Prior to circulating them, your bookmobile allows you to deliver both the material (in the form of your eReader or tablet) and a practical lesson on how to use it directly to your patron. Updates to a lent device's content or operating system can also occur via the bookmobile. Finally, use of a mobile ILS or a provisional library card can allow you to create immediate borrowers of your digital collection.

FINAL THOUGHTS

Clearly there are a myriad of ways to tackle outreach in support of your library's digital collection. Many of these can be adjusted to fit both budget and situation. With time and perhaps a bit of trial and error, you will discover the approach that works best for your organization. As is often the case, the staff you choose to assign to the task can have a great bearing on its success. Outreach staff members function as library ambassadors. They work with not only individual members of your public but also organizations and entities that can collectively have a powerful effect on your library. By projecting an image your organization would be proud of, you can ensure these effects are beneficial ones.

Chapter 6

Saving Money and Justifying Expenses

In the previous chapters, we've examined ways to train staff, instruct patrons, and promote services using a variety of techniques. There are, of course, costs associated with most methods. Technology is often costly. In a time of shrinking budgets, how can you maximize your investment? Are you prepared to justify expenses to your library board of trustees and your public at large? Will you be able to show that the money was spent wisely?

WAYS OF SAVING MONEY

Saving Money No. 1: Extending the Life of a Device

One of the more expensive components in service to a digital collection is the various tablets and eReaders you will use for staff and patron instruction. Maximizing the lifespan of these devices can help make an initial investment serve as a foundation on which to build. It may then be possible to reduce future costs by turning to maintenance rather than outright replacement each year. There are simple ways to extend the lifespan of a device.

There is no surer way to blow through a technology budget than lose your equipment to damage or theft. Recall our security mounts, tethers, and enclosures discussed in Chapter One and Chapter Two. More often than not, the price of these items was below the replacement cost of the devices they protected. It may seem clichéd, but sometimes you need to spend money in order to save money. In a similar vein, you should strongly consider purchasing warranties on your equipment, such as AppleCare for iOS devices. While you may debate the cost of a warranty on a device for personal use, the expected wear and tear on an item that is lent or otherwise used by multiple members of your staff and public makes it a no-brainer.

In light of these facts, I must reiterate the importance of making the maintenance of equipment a priority. Security equipment used on public displays for both patrons and staff members need to be checked regularly. Warranties on equipment should be filed away, lest you find yourself unable to call them in when necessary. Similarly, examine any applicable warranties on your security equipment itself. You may find that they themselves offer some guarantee against theft or tampering. This can provide you with an added layer of insurance. Even more passive security, such as screen guards and cases, may do the same, though in a more limited scope. Even after the life of a device has ended, there remains the possibility that you can reuse security equipment, representing another money saver.

Having the best and newest devices is often a luxury more than a requirement. If your intent is to expose your patrons to the newest technology, then you will find yourself continually buying new gadgets. If, however, your primary focus is on the promotion and use of your library's digital collection, you need not constantly replace equipment. In this case, your focus should be on software, rather than hardware.

When we think about mobile devices accessing the library's collection, we think of compatibility. What devices work with your collection? Is there an app for your patrons' devices? More often than not, compatibility rests with a device's operating system and not its model. For example, eBook vendor 3M Cloud Library offers an iOS app. This app is compatible for iPads and iPhones that are running iOS 6 or higher. The full list of Apple devices that can run iOS 6 are the iPhone 3GS, iPhone 4, iPhone 4S, iPad 2, iPad 3, and iPod touch 4th generation (OSXDaily 2012). A number of these devices are several years old. The iPhone 3GS was released on June 8, 2009 (Apple Press Info 2009). All those years later, this device and others are still capable of using this particular digital collection.

Again, compatibility is your foremost concern. Do the devices you own support the operating system and, by extension, the digital collection your library offers? As time passes and your devices age, new operating systems will be released. If your library owned an original model iPad, it would be unable to download anything after iOS 5. As a result, you would be unable to install the aforementioned 3M Cloud Library app. What happens then? In this scenario, you would lose access to your digital collection. This and other same model devices could no longer be used to walk a patron through the use of your digital collection. This means it cannot be used at your reference desk to model the patron's experience, making in-person, phone, and e-mail assistance much more difficult. Service-oriented classes could not be conducted with it. Do you then discard it?

Before you lose hope with your outmoded device, consider how much has changed on the hardware side? If we continue to look at iOS, the iPad has gotten thinner, faster, and more powerful as new models are released. Still, many of the same features are in place or easily identifiable, such as the home button, volume controls, and power. Looking at the operating system, while it may not support the installation of a library-related app, it bears more than a passing resemblance to earlier versions of iOS.

If on navigating the desktop most settings and Wi-Fi are still largely similar to the newest operating system, it may still be used at some level for staff and patron assistance. In terms of basic mobile device orientation, you may find it can still adequately cover core lessons while you budget for a replacement. Lessons could still include navigating settings, touch gestures, installing/deleting apps, and connecting to a wireless network. If you were loath to lend a device because of cost concerns, perhaps those will go away as it approaches the end of life. Such a device could be preloaded with whatever content is still compatible.

You may also consider repurposing a device for uses besides your digital collection. Looking first at staff use, perhaps a tablet can now serve as digital signage in support of other library collections and services. Can it run a mobile version of your integrated library system (ILS) on it? If so, you can use it to support your outreach efforts as outlined in Chapter Five. If not, you may still run your basic library catalog off it, making it an effective tool librarians can take with them into the stacks when assisting your patrons. Many tablets have high-quality built-in cameras. Why not put them to use in photographing library programs and events? As they are web-connected devices, you can easily upload photos directly to your library's social media sites.

With regards to repurposing devices for your patrons, consider using them in programming, particularly with children. Adding some basic educational games can allow you to offer tablet play time-type programming, where patrons are exposed to age-appropriate games. You can also offer digital art classes using tablets with doodle, sketch, and painting apps, not to mention photography. In both cases, there are numerous available apps that should be compatible with older versions of an Android or iOS operating system.

Saving Money No. 2: Pay Attention to New Releases of Operating Systems

When managing costs, it is helpful to develop a schedule of expected maintenance. Such a schedule will allow you to responsibly plan and budget for the future. Having seen the importance operating systems hold with regards to the effectiveness of library-owned devices, this should play a major role in your planning. Upon their release, new iOS devices come with the most up-to-date operating system available. Android tablets may have a range of versions of their operating system available to them, depending on the device specifications. It is important to try and purchase Android tablets that come standard with the newest version of the Android operating system.

The ideal purchase occurs shortly after the release. In this way, you know that a device's operating system will have the longest possible shelf life. Rarely does the ideal actually take place. Many gadgets are released during the holidays. Depending on how your library's fiscal year is structured, this may or may not align with it. If caught in the lurch, do some prior research.

Identify when the newest iOS, Android, Kindle, or other device is expected to be released. Keep a lookout for upcoming operating system releases. You need not be a spymaster. There are several websites that you can check in on for periodic updates. Mashable (2015) and PC Mag (2015) both offer good general information on upcoming operating system releases, among other technology-oriented news. If you want to specifically keep tabs on Android and iOS, you can turn to some of these resources:

For Apple

Mac Rumors (www.macrumors.com) is a site that, while it does deal with rumors, also offers substantiated information on Apple devices and operating systems. For more of a traditional source, you can subscribe to Apple Magazine or visit Apple's "Hot News" section at http://www.apple.com/hotnews.

For Android

Android Central (http://www.androidcentral.com) offers a vast amount of news, reviews, and information relating to both devices and the Android operating system. If you are seeking a more official source, you can follow the Android-specific blog maintained by Google at http://officialandroid.blogspot.com.

Once you begin purchasing devices compatible with your digital collection, assemble a list of them. With an ear to the ground, take notice of any major upcoming operating system releases applicable to your devices and mark the date. When you discover one, you need to find out how, if at all, it will impact you. Check to see if your device will be able to install it. If you cannot, this will impact your ability to offer programs around it. If the device is located within your gadget petting zoo, understand you'll be showcasing a soon-to-be dated experience.

Next, you'll need to contact any vendors supplying you with digital media for these devices. Will they still offer support for previous operating systems or will you and your patrons be required to have the newest or newer one in order to access the collection? They likely will not have an immediate answer for you. They, like you, will be reacting to this announcement. Once you do have answers, you should have several months (hopefully) during which to plan a new purchase, if that is in order. You can likewise develop a responsible transition for a device that may become outmoded. If the release of a new device is set to coincide with this operating system, you may also wish to plan to purchase it as a means of maximizing the shelf life.

Saving Money No. 3: Use Devices for Multiple Purposes

We looked at extending the value of your equipment purchases through repurposing. Let's now look at multipurposing. If you were to take on a number of the options outlined in this book to promote use of your digital collection, what might that entail? Tablets and eReaders for staff training. Tablets and eReaders for device lending. Tablets and eReaders for patron instruction. Tablets and eReaders for a gadget petting zoo. Just because separate services might require four devices and then three devices, and so on, it does not mean this has to be handled cumulatively. With a bit of planning, you can instead multipurpose the same set of devices to fulfill many of these roles.

Start by identifying when devices will be in use and, more importantly, when *should* they be in use? You may wish to consider your gadget petting zoo as a passive promotional tool to be used when devices are otherwise not in use. If the station is set up to provide them with power supply, they can sit there indefinitely, offering a hands-on experience to patrons when they're not actively serving another purpose. This works well if the station is located near your reference desk. If a question arises, which requires the use of one of the devices in your petting zoo, a staff member can simply go over and unlock one. Upon assisting your patron, the device is simply returned to its security fixture and plugged back in.

If you conduct your staff training in cycles, you can provide patron instruction on an alternate schedule, eliminating the need for two separate collections of equipment. Now it is likely that you would want very different setups on the same devices depending on whether they are being used with patrons or staff, not to mention their purpose with each. Here is where cloud computing is our ally.

Cloud computing is simply the storage and accessing of data and programs over the Internet instead of your device's hard drive (PC Mag 2015). On tablets and eReaders, content including apps and media that you purchase and download is tied to your account. By maintaining separate accounts based around an intended purpose, it is possible to use the cloud to quickly switch devices over.

For example, imagine you were using an Android tablet both in a gadget petting zoo and while teaching a class. In this instance, you would have two distinct Google accounts that you would use—let's call them "class@gmail.com" and "pettingzoo@gmail.com." When teaching your class, you would have the tablet authorized with your class account. This account would have whatever apps facilitated your class, if this were a topic that was touched on. At the end of the class, you would want to return the tablet to your petting zoo. At this point, you would go into setting and remove the class account (Nexus 2015). Once removed, you could then add the existing petting zoo account, allowing you to restore your data, such as downloaded apps. Similarly, the iCloud feature on Apple devices allows you to restore from a backup (Apple 2015c). Maintaining distinct iTunes accounts will allow you the same flexibility to switch the intended use of your devices.

Saving Money No. 4: Coordinate Purchases, Share Equipment

We've seen how reusing the same devices for multiple purposes can stretch your budget. Why not share devices between other libraries to similarly maximize your investment? If your library is part of a consortium, you can easily benefit from a coordinated order of equipment. An immediate benefit of a coordinated order is the potential for bulk purchasing discounts. Many vendors will offer a not unsubstantial discount depending on the quantity ordered. This type of discount extends beyond just the devices themselves.

Screen protectors, security enclosures, tethers, and mounts may all be subject to bulk discounts. Additionally, you may find that apps and digital media can also qualify. Apple runs a volume purchasing plan that qualifies some content for a discount if purchased in numbers of 20 or more (Apple 2015c). The combined cost savings on all these items can quickly add up. Once you've purchased your discounted equipment, how best do you proceed? In many ways, this depends on how robust your purchase was and how you wish to operate.

If a purchase was substantial enough, then a collection may be distributed to branch libraries. Here, the savings is simply that of purchasing in bulk. While this gives individual libraries the most flexibility, it entails a cost that could be reduced. If you are willing to sacrifice some flexibility in order to save additional money, then your purchase can instead be used to form a pool collection of devices shared among member libraries. Depending on the size of your consortium, you can create one or several sets of devices with specific functions in mind. To avoid unnecessary complications, it is recommended that these devices are not multipurpose and instead retain one consistent account.

In practice, your consortium or main branch would determine the purpose of the pool collection of devices. They would then assign accounts accordingly. This might mean one or several sets of devices for staff training, patron instruction, device lending, gadget petting zoos, and so on. Once established, they could then remain on location until requested by individual branches.

You will not need identical numbers of collections. A gadget petting zoo could very well operate as a single collection that is lent to member libraries for a few weeks at a time. In the case of a petting zoo, it may work best to lend it furniture and all. A simple desk or table on iron casters can operate as a mobile petting zoo that is simply brought to a library, wheeled into place, and plugged in. Such a setup will reduce wear on security equipment, as they can become damaged from being constantly disassembled and reassembled.

Centralizing the staff training stations described in Chapter Two may also seem desirable, although it comes with trade-offs. On the other hand, you can reduce the quantity needed by eliminating transit time of this collection between libraries. Instead, the stations may always be available for use at one central location. Recall, however, that one of the benefits of these stations is the self-guided nature of them. The ability of a staff member to simply head to a back office and train when the opportunity presents itself is a convenience that may be lost if they instead need to travel some miles away to another location. Depending on the size of your service district and the spacing between libraries, it could be that the station is placed in areas central to multiple branches.

What about the Stand-Alone Libraries?

As a stand-alone library, the natural avenues for coordinated orders and resource sharing may not exist, but this doesn't mean they can't. Other libraries around you are likely facing the same pressures as your organization. Working collaboratively to tackle your problems can reduce costs on each of your libraries. As you are distinct entities, not all models we discussed will work.

Even assuming your libraries share the same ILS, lending between your organizations may be prohibited or overly complicated. This likely eliminates any device lending to your patrons. Unless there is a high degree of trust and coordination between libraries, it is inadvisable that you share any account information. A joint collection of tablets and eReaders could easily be shared for the purposes of training staff members and patrons. Simply splitting the cost with a second library should allow you to offer regular training and instruction on a regular basis.

Much like the repurposed devices, each organization will want to keep separate accounts. When devices are in your possession, they can be authorized with these credentials, gaining you access to any content you may have purchased or otherwise downloaded. At the point when you are ready to transfer the devices to another organization, you should remove your account information prior to doing so. Indeed, a full factory reset would be advisable.

This type of resource sharing can be extended to more than just equipment. Developing staff and patron resources can be time-consuming. If your libraries share the same vendors for your digital collection, why not share your tutorials, training packets, support sites, and so forth? Doing so can allow you to quickly assemble these resources and save time in the long term by lessening the burden of maintenance.

If you decide to engage in such a venture, there are several issues you will need to address. Library-maintained resources have the advantage of specificity. You will be able to instruct staff and patrons on the unique way a service operates within your library. This includes using screenshots representative of your collection that may be branded and arranged to your own preference. You will make note of methods of authentication that are specific to your library, such as choosing your branch from a dropdown, entering a barcode, username, or needing to enter a pin/password. Lending rules may be decided on an individual basis by participating libraries.

If all these customizations exist, there is a strong possibility they don't perfectly align with the library you're partnering with. You should investigate and list these differences prior to creating shared resources. Are these differences irreconcilable? Ideally, you can use more general graphics and descriptions to create an effective resource for all involved. If you decide to go through with the venture, ensure that you not only divide the initial creation, but the maintenance as well. An up-to-date resource won't be current for long without occasional upkeep. Each participating library should assign a point person responsible for quality control. They should be contacted whenever a need for an update is identified.

Saving Money No. 5: Donations and Grant Programs

Surely the best way to save money is not to pay at all. With some persistence, it is possible to secure free equipment, software, and support. Consider a gadget petting zoo. Through it, you are giving your patrons a hands-on experience with new technology. What you are also doing, by choosing what to display, is advertising particular brands and models of devices. You may find that some companies recognize this opportunity and are willing to invest in your library.

Before going defunct in 2014 (Sony Reader Store 2014), Sony saw libraries as an opportunity to expose patrons to their eReader. They actively courted libraries willing to display their collection of devices. My library was likewise interested, and in 2010, the Community Library was one of 30 inaugural libraries in their "Reader Library Program" (Geek 2010). In this program, we received numerous benefits at no cost.

For starters, we received in-person workshop-style training from a Sony Reader representative. The staff was instructed on the hardware and software of several models of Sony eReaders. The download process was explained and individual settings explored. This training was invaluable. At the time, our experience with eBooks and eReaders was limited, at best. Through this program, we were able to schedule several workshops, exposing a large number of staff members to an emerging technology. We were shortly thereafter able to use this base of knowledge to improve our own staff training curriculum and our ability to instruct patrons. In addition to this training, we received further benefits.

We were given a floor display of eReaders. This floor display was a large metal stand, containing two attached Sony Readers, including a smaller pocket edition. The eReaders were programmed to run in a kiosk mode. This kiosk mode operated much like a screensaver, outlining the features of each device. When in use, they simply returned to a standard setting. Each device was preloaded with some sample content. The kiosk software allowed them to easily return to their programmed settings, preventing unauthorized changes to the devices.

Attached to the display was a series of booklets on three-ring binders, which gave further product information. This included the basic operation of an eReader, settings, and navigation—much of what you'd expect to see in a handout during a class! Along the top, was a signage that enticed patrons to "try me." All the wiring was contained within, meaning a single wire running to an outlet could power the entire display.

Regarding the devices themselves, we were entitled to a bulk purchasing program that came with steep discounts. We were able to take advantage of these savings to assemble a collection for staff training as well as institute our first eReader lending program at a very affordable price. This discount included cases and (prior to the backlit eReader) light attachments.

All this was achieved by partnering with a company that saw it in their best interest to work with libraries. In absence of an active program as described above, you may need to do some footwork. Most major companies offer some form of community outreach or social responsibility programs you may be able to take advantage of. This possibility becomes more feasible if the company has a manufacturing or distribution facility nearby, as you can avoid much of the bureaucracy and instead deal with a local representative. You can also choose to think even smaller.

Rather than deal with a device's manufacturer, which is far less likely to have a local presence, why not target local sellers? This could be a chain like Best Buy or a mom and pop store. These entities are far more interested in promoting their own store or brand over individual devices. Promising some sort of public recognition may be enough to effectively solicit a donation. For starters, a thank you in the newsletter serves as a nice piece of advertising. If they are contributing devices to a gadget petting zoo, a placard or signage that indicates who donated the equipment is also a good incentive. As it costs nothing to ask, what do you have to lose?

If your organization has a Friends of the Library nonprofit, they can help fund the promotion of your digital collection. Book sales, raffles, and other fundraising efforts can bring in much needed money outside the library's budget. This can be helpful when initially purchasing technology, as your budget may not yet be adjusted to a new approach you plan on taking. Additionally, your initial start-up costs tend to be higher, as you must first build a foundation of software, devices, and other hardware at the outset.

Volunteers

This book outlines an approach to training that relies on the staff assisting your patrons. In some libraries, the staff simply doesn't exist and they must rely heavily on volunteers. If you find yourself in that situation, or otherwise need to ease the burden on the staff, it is possible to pass on some one-on-one tech assistance to a group of volunteers. Indeed, libraries both large and small have relied on this method, particularly using their teen patrons.

For example, the Fairport Library offers a "Teen Tech Tutor Team" (Fairport Public Library 2015a), where teen volunteers are able to offer patrons basic technology assistance in exchange for community service credit. Teens first obtain parental permission before filling out an application, which in part outlines their current familiarity with a variety of technologies, as well as their availability (Fairport Public Library 2015b). The volunteers then undergo mandatory training before they are able to assist library patrons. The assistance covers mobile device use in addition to computer and Internet basics.

As a cost saver, volunteers are an attractive option. They do come with drawbacks. For starters, you are very much at the mercy of their availability. Once trained, volunteers do end up moving on, making turnover an issue. As volunteers leave, you will need to train a new batch, which may be manageable if it's cyclical, such as graduation time. If a number of trainers are lost on an irregular basis, it may prove disruptive to the operation of your library. The Brooklyn Public Library System requires that volunteers commit to a six-month term (Brooklyn Public Library 2015), although that can prove difficult to enforce. Additionally, a staff member does need to be on hand in a supervisory role to ensure appointments are carried out safely and appropriately.

Free Content

With the availability of public domain eBooks, it is possible to supplement your digital collection with third-party sites. In some cases, you can download some content permanently. For example, Project Gutenberg (2015) offers 49,000 eBook titles for download in both Kindle and ePub format, making them accessible to tablets and all brands of eReaders. OpenLibrary. org has over a million ePub and PDF titles that can be borrowed, up to five at a time. For a focus on Kindle format, BookLending.com matches eBook borrowers with lenders, facilitating the Kindle Lending feature (BookLending.com 2015).

With the free downloaded content, you can provide content to a circulating collection of devices. At the Community Library, we have begun to use public domain eBooks to ease the financial burden of carrying multiple copies of the classics. Instead, we devote several eReaders to housing hundreds of these titles. We can separately provide the URL to this content for those not wishing to borrow a device. This has allowed us to reduce the number of physical copies we are purchasing, providing us with significant savings.

Consider a giveaway of free eBooks as part of a library promotion. Prizes can be expensive, but with some creativity, you can reduce costs by relying on free, permanent downloads from sites like Project Gutenberg. Library-branded flash drives can be ordered in bulk inexpensively. It is then a small matter to copy over several dozen classic titles in PDF format. Rather than a tchotchke, you can give patrons an entire digital library.

While free, permanently downloaded content is great, what about sites that offer a free lending model? You may have concerns over pointing patrons in the direction of some of these sites that can be viewed as competition. There are several important points to be made here. Unless your library has the budget to supply patrons with all the content they want, you're going to fall short of their borrowing needs, unless you provide supplementary materials. Often, this can be a short-term fix, buying you the time to build a more comprehensive collection. Restricting information has never been in the library's interest. By evaluating and then curating these sites for your patrons, you are fulfilling your role as an information specialist. Patrons will often find these sites on their own—wouldn't you prefer it was you they found them from?

JUSTIFYING EXPENSES

We've seen ways to stretch a budget in support of your library's digital collection. While applying some of these techniques can ensure that you've spent money responsibly, it can also help to have other forms of justification for your library board and your patrons as a whole. Doing so can help prepare you for any questions that may arise in response to particular services and their associated expenditures. As a precursor, you must first decide what a library card is worth to you.

We commonly direct this line of thinking toward our patrons. Let's turn it inward for a moment. From device lending to one-on-one and group instruction, these services and equipment can be quite expensive. The goal is, of course, to get patrons to use your digital collection. For some, this may be the only way they can borrow materials from the library. As technology continues to evolve, this scenario only becomes more prevalent as media becomes increasingly digital.

For libraries that receive funding on a cardholder basis, such as contract patrons, this number is very quantifiable. In this scenario, each patron represents an actual dollar amount. For most, however, the number is far more nebulous. When you consider that the intent of posters, flyers, newsletters, signage, and displays we traditionally use is to attract use of the library, it becomes pretty clear that we assign a high value. When viewed through this lens, your investments will prove proportionate. Looking specifically at individual uses of resources, what cases can be made?

The One-on-One Appointment

One-on-one appointments represent a staff-intensive endeavor. Time is, of course, money, and depending on the staff assigned, it can represent a significant expense. While assisting patrons in this fashion may be costly, it can also result in a large return on investment. In my experience, patrons that take advantage of this service become power users of the library. Once they are able to move to a measure of comfort with their device and your collection, they grow in confidence. Once comfortable with one form of digital media, they wish to try others. They attend other library technology classes. Essentially, these appointments serve as a gateway to library digital services and digital literacy at large.

These power users tend to be intensely loyal. They develop personal relationships with instructors, often requesting them by name. They also tell their friends and family of these services. We reach an incredible number of patrons through word of mouth. Surely these types of patron experiences aid you when the budget is up for a vote?

Gadget Petting Zoos

If you've received your gadgets free of charge, there's probably no need for justification. On the other hand, if you've made a substantial investment in the devices, what are you getting for your money? Here's where a bit of statistics keeping can go a long way. Informally, you can keep track of patrons visiting the station. This might be a check that occurs at regular intervals or whenever the staff notices a patron interacting with it. This is easier to do if your station is located near the reference desk. Whenever staff interaction is required, you can track the reference questions you answer as a result.

Even without staff assistance, you will be surprised by the transactions a station generates. Just four patron interactions a day will translate to over 1,000 annually. If you are housing devices used for staff and patron instruction in your petting zoo during slack time, you truly are receiving an excellent value.

Staff Instruction

The investment in time and equipment should be among the easier justifications to make. You cannot reasonably expect the staff to assist patrons on devices that they haven't had the time and opportunity to learn. Surely, staff members are expected to be proficient with the basics of computer use and performing web-based searches. Increasingly, tablets, smartphones, and other mobile devices are now the way your patrons are accessing the Internet (ComScore 2014). If your library is expected to adapt to change and invest in digital media, then a small collection of devices for staff training must be understood as a critical need.

Patron Instruction

In a smaller library, this collection and the one used to train the staff are likely one and the same. Using devices for patron instruction can quickly recuperate their cost. Nearly all libraries offer some form of computer instruction. Consider these mobile device- and service-oriented classes as the new computer instruction. Think of the cost of bringing in an outside instructor on a per class basis. Just a few classes can quickly run you hundreds into thousands of dollars. Conducting these types of programs in-house with library-owned devices is a true cost saver.

Device Lending

In many ways, device lending is a luxury. Ensure that you are engaging in simpler, more direct support of your digital collection before taking this service on. Ironically, the cost of such a program is an argument in support of it. The expensive nature of tablets and eReaders has many of your patrons view them as luxuries. That the library can absorb this cost and provide an experience to large numbers of patrons who might otherwise not have the opportunity is important. For some, this may be the only way to consume library digital media. The existence of eBook exclusive titles means patrons without these devices might not have access to some materials. Finally, this collection of circulating devices often serves as a precursor to patrons buying one of their own and becoming regular users of your digital collection.

Patron Group Instruction

Simply looking at this instruction as a standard class generally justifies the expense, particularly with the basic mobile device-oriented classes. In my experience, basic courses on the iPad, Android devices, Kindle Fire, and eReaders are of high interest and are well attended. In particular, centering these classes during pre- and post-holidays can capitalize on patron buying habits. Service-oriented programs can generate interest when a service is new. Over time, interest can wane, if the classes are spaced too closely together. When a service appears established, you can turn to one-on-one appointments to address a diminished need on an individual basis.

When you look at the one-time cost of purchasing a tablet, it is not dissimilar from that of paying an outside individual to teach a single class. Investing in your own collection of devices will allow you to offer classes on a regular basis. Even considering staffing costs, you will quickly come out ahead. Unlike crafts, there are no consumable material costs. Once the initial purchase is made, the more it's used the better—allowing you to demonstrate a very efficient cost per patron in these classes.

Bending the Cost Curve

When your library purchases materials, you allocate budget around the expected use. Use statistics to inform one's spending. One of the more common calculations libraries make when evaluating their collection is cost per circulation. Simply put, it measures how much an item costs, divided by how many times it has been used in its lifetime. If you were to spend $50 on a book and it's circulated 100 times, your cost per circulation would be 50 cents. If, on the other hand, you spent $25 on a book and it circulated 25 times, your cost per circulation would be $1 or twice the cost. Clearly, there is more to measure than just the initial purchase price of an item.

Looking more broadly at your collection as a whole, let's consider two separate approaches. Imagine you had a budget of $10,000 for your digital collection. For simplicity's sake, we'll say your focus is entirely on eBooks and the model is one copy/one user. In other words, you purchase titles on an individual basis. They are then checked out by a patron and are unavailable until returned (Overdrive Media Station 2015). In your first approach, you would spend that money entirely on the collection itself.

If a copy of an eBook cost you $50, you would have assembled a collection of 200 copies. At the end of the year, your collection has a circulation of 5000 checkouts. Dividing your holdings, your eBook investment had a per circulation cost of $2 a checkout ($10,000 divided by 5,000 checkouts). Your average eBook copy circulated 25 times (5,000 checkouts divided by 200 copies).

In a second approach you would again have $10,000 to spend. Instead of using it all on eBooks, you set aside $15,000 to invest in a small collection of devices for staff and patron instruction. A sample expenditure might look like this:

Devices:

iOS:
  iPad Mini 3 with 16 GB of Storage (Wi-Fi only) $399
  Two year AppleCare Warranty: $99
  VGA to Lightning Adapter: $49
  Total: $547 (Apple Store 2015)

Android:
  Eight-inch Samsung Galaxy Tab A: $229
  Samsung Two Year Extended Coverage Plan: $69.99 (Samsung 2015a)
  MicroHDMI to VGA Adapter: $39.99 (Samsung 2015b)
  Total: $338.98

Kindle:
  Kindle Fire HDX (Without special offers): $215
  Two Year Warranty and Accident Protection: $54.99 (Amazon 2015b, Kindle Fire)
  Amazon Kindle Paperwhite eReader (without special offers) $139.00
  Two Year Warranty and Accident Protection: $29.99 (Amazon 2015b, Kindle Fire)
  Total: $438.98

NOOK:
  NOOK GlowLight eReader: $99
  Two Year Extended Protection Plan: $19.99 (Barnes and Noble 2015)
  Total: $119.99
  Grand Total: $1,444.95

Coming in just under the target budget, for devices we are able to provide a basic collection on which to instruct patrons and staff. Android, iOS, and Kindle tablets are covered, and the adapters we budgeted for will allow you to connect them to a standard laptop projector. Warranties will insure you against damage, giving this collection at least a two-year lifespan on the hardware side. Armed with these devices, you begin instructing your staff and patrons. With your remaining $8,500, you build your collection of eBooks.

Using the same metrics as before, at $50 per title, you collection is 170 copies ($8,500 divided by $50 a copy). If your staff and patron instruction can boost your circulation by just 15 percent, you will have already done better than having spent the entire $10,000 budget on content.

Your previous base checkout was 25 circs per eBook copy. A 15 percent increase would be $25 \times 1.15 = 28.75$ checkouts per copy.

In this model, your collection is 175 copies. Multiplying that by your checkouts per copy would be $175 \times 28.75 = 5,031.25$ total checkouts.

Put another way, to break-even in this hypothetical model is as follows:

Our original cost per circulation was estimated at $2 per checkout. We now have 25 less circulating items, but our investment was still $10,000. To reach the same $2 per checkout, as before, we would still need 5,000 checkouts per year. We would now, however, need an average of 28.57 checkouts per item (5,000 checkouts divided by 175 copies).

Taking advantage of the device training our $1,500 investment allowed, if staff can help push an average of 4 more circulations per item per year, bringing us to 29 checkouts per eBook copy, they've effectively reduced the cost per checkout and increased the total digital circulation. The total checkouts at 29 circulations per eBook would be 5,075 ($175 \times 29 = 5,075$). The average per circulation cost for each eBook would now be $1.97 per checkout ($10,000 divided by 5,075 checkouts).

Even using an extremely pessimistic take on the impact of a well-trained staff and an informed public, your organization will come out ahead in an investment in mobile devices. In reality, the support services you will be able to offer your patrons should yield even better results. Group instruction on devices can build the mobile device skills that are prerequisite to using your collection. Service specific classes will allow you to rapidly build an established user base. With devices on hand, you can create accurate support resources using screenshots that serve as walkthroughs. When placed on your website, these resources can assist patrons who cannot make it to your library.

A knowledgeable staff will be capable of hand-selling your collection to patrons with confidence. When a patron struggles, the ability to receive in-person assistance can be the difference between getting past a problem and giving up on the library's collection. Building on this experience, some staff will take on the task of advanced troubleshooting or tailored lessons in one-on-one settings. With devices making all this possible, a small investment in them seems not only reasonable but also easily justifiable.

Responsible use of these devices can mean a reduced impact to your budget in subsequent fiscal years, as you won't need to replace all equipment outright. The continued boon that this resource will bestow going forward further enhances the value of your initial investment. You then have the option to redirect funds back into building your digital collection or perhaps expand the support you give to it. If year-one expenditures allow for you to train the staff and offer classes, an investment can be made in security fixtures to house your devices in a gadget petting zoo. Alternately, you instead use funds to create a kiosk.

Taking a Measured Approach

Perhaps your library is extremely well funded and adventurous. In this happy circumstance, you can simply purchase all the devices, enclosures, software, and supporting materials outlined in this book. More often than not, the reality is a library's funds are limited. A library board or administration may be hesitant to spend money on technology. It is human nature to want assurances. While you cannot predict the future, you can point to past success as an argument for further resources. It can therefore be helpful to take a measured approach. Without initial funding for software and equipment, how can you proceed?

If administration is risk-averse, start with the least expensive methods you can undertake in support of your digital collection. Looking at marketing, create flyers advertising your services. Lean heavily on social media to help get the word out, excluding paid advertisements for the time being. Place signage in high-traffic areas of the library. If your website has a slide show or otherwise features certain content, locate information on your collection here. When your newsletter comes out, give priority placement to library digital media. The combined effect of these low-cost approaches should be increased interest in your collection. When these patrons come asking questions, how can the staff initially respond in the absence of fully funded support services?

If initial funding leaves you without a core set of devices to train with, providing patron support can truly be daunting. In this unfortunate scenario, you may need to rely on the staff's personal experience at the outset. Check to see what devices are personally owned by the staff. You may find that an informal core collection exists. While you cannot reasonably expect staff members to make their own personal devices available to their coworkers at large, they can aid your support services in other ways. Perhaps these staff members can assist in an open house, showing how a service works to their coworkers. Their own device need not leave their hands, particularly if you have an inexpensive adapter to connect to a projector. These same staff members can help assemble staff and patron walkthroughs. Even if a staff member may not be able to create the resource themselves (such as it not being within their job responsibilities), they can provide the all-important screenshots of the experience of using a digital collection. Those screenshots can lay the groundwork for handouts and web based resources staff and patrons can rely on.

What is clearly lacking in this scenario is hands-on mobile device instruction. This is a glaring deficiency that must ultimately be addressed in order for you to succeed. Until this happens, there are ways to mitigate the difficulties staff and, by extension, patrons will face. Much like the staff proficiency chart we outlined in Chapter One, you can assemble a chart showing who among your frontline staff members has personal familiarity with mobile technology, albeit absent formal training. For example, if someone owned a Kindle eReader and was generally familiar with how it worked, you would record this. Once you have created your list, you can better see where staff comfort lies. From a staffing perspective you can adjust desk schedules in an attempt to increase coverage for library digital media questions. If adjustments to schedule are not possible, having a chart available for the staff should at least allow you to call for backup when a patron's question cannot be answered due to inexperience with the device on hand.

What I have described here is far from ideal. It will likely result in staff and patron frustration. It is up to you to effectively communicate these hardships to administration so that they may be remedied. At your reference desk, you commonly record patron interactions, such as reference and informational questions. How detailed is your record keeping? Does it specifically categorize this data? Keeping track of the type and frequency of questions pertaining to your digital collection will allow you to demonstrate need.

Aside from specific reference interactions, do you maintain a suggestion box? Documenting patron requests for classes, one-on-one appointments, and other support services can help make the case for these resources. Often, patrons will become aware of these services from friends and family frequenting other libraries. Look to your peers. If your digital services compare unfavorably with libraries of similar size and budget, this fact can be used to bolster an argument for more support. If patrons are unhappy with their experience, point them in the direction of appropriate outlets, such as speaking to an administrator or attending a board of trustees meeting. Care should be taken to ensure that this doesn't take on an antagonistic appearance, but rather that you are relaying patron concerns through standard library channels.

Proceeding in this fashion will allow you to make the most of scarce resources. It will, however, also force you to be reactive rather than proactive. Essentially, you will do what you can with what you have, while gathering evidence for further action. While this can be a difficult situation to be in, there are positive aspects.

As much as possible, libraries want to be reflective of their community. When you make the support of your digital collection driven by demonstrated community needs, you are insulating yourself against accusations of unnecessary expenditures. Your purchases, to a large degree, are patron driven and fulfill requests for classes and knowledgeable staff. Rather than going out on a limb, you are catching up to your peers in meeting the needs of a twenty-first-century library. In the face of all these data, you should be able to prioritize funds in support of your digital collection.

Conclusion

Final Thoughts

Libraries face numerous challenges in the twenty-first century. One of the most pressing is managing the shift of traditional media to digital. Following the approaches outlined in this book will allow you to meet these challenges head-on, making the most of your library's collection and turning a challenge into an opportunity for growth as an organization.

COMBATING THE STEREOTYPE

Our patrons and the public at large still strongly associate the word library with books. Far fewer connect the library to technology. Offering mobile device classes to your patrons redefines the library as a place of literacy to include digital literacy. You are framing your staff members as the experts in this field. As patrons learn mobile competencies from the library staff, they are likely to return to the library to continue their education. Rather than view the library as a depository of the old, you are building an expectation that the library offers the latest technology.

DEALING WITH THE COMPETITION

When it comes to traditional media, the library is well situated to succeed. The First Sale Doctrine provides "that an individual who knowingly purchases a copy of a copyrighted work from the copyright holder receives the right to sell, display or otherwise dispose of that particular copy, notwithstanding the interests of the copyright owner" (Office of the US Attorneys 1854). In effect, once we've purchased materials, we can resell or, in our case, lend them out without violating copyright. It is this provision of law that allows libraries to circulate books, DVDs, CDs, and all other forms of copyrighted media. Using this provision, libraries are able to amass collections of the most popular materials requested by our patrons. Unfortunately, the same is not true of digital media.

Digital media is considered to be licensed software. This allows publishers to place restrictions on content that do not exist on their physical counterparts. While digital media companies such as Hulu, Netflix, and Amazon and others are able to offer a simple, easy-to-use purchasing experience, library lending faces many hurdles, some intentional. Digital rights management software, made to protect copyright, often has the effect of making the borrowing experience difficult and overly complicated.

Third-party software may need to be installed and separate accounts created. This can differ radically from the sign-in and checkout/play/download model of our competitors.

To help level the playing field, we must do what a large company cannot. We must utilize the personal touch. Having the trained staff available by phone, e-mail, and in person can help patrons navigate your collection, effectively removing obstacles to its use. A one-on-one technology appointment can meet the needs of our patrons that are most likely to experience difficulty. If we can strip away all the ways our service is more difficult to use, what we have left is a comparable, free alternative to our for-profit competition.

Far from running from your competitors, the mobile device instruction for patrons outlined in this book allows you to co-opt them. While the competition may, at least now, enjoy an easier shopping experience, there are some members of your community that find even that to be confusing. In-person support can be hard to find outside the library. Where it does exist, it tends to be focused on using that device and its associated services. Apple doesn't benefit from its customers using Netflix! Unlike these media companies and device manufacturers, our loyalties lie only with our patrons.

When you instruct patrons on the use of their mobile device either one on one or in groups, their questions often turn to the use of third-party services and content. When your approach is one of honesty and openness, you instill trust in your patrons. At the end of these classes, you distribute information on compatible library digital collections, allowing them to make an informed decision on how they wish to use their devices. Even if they decide to use a competitor's service, they are likely to return to you with future questions. Are these encounters not a desired use of your library? This continued relationship allows the patron time to revisit a collection that may have improved its content or ease of use.

RETRAINING STAFF FOR TWENTY-FIRST-CENTURY CHALLENGES

As media goes increasingly digital, libraries have begun offering access to these materials. As with any new technology, these access points are hardly static. Digital collections continuously change in appearance and procedure. Formats may vary. What is more, new services appear, offering the same or different material types. At the same time, these materials are being consumed, in large part, by mobile devices that your staff may have no experience with. In response, this book uses an adaptable training model that addresses this staff skill deficiency with the rapid nature of change in mind, while at the same time minimizing the burden on your library.

By breaking staff training into three distinct levels, you need not train everyone on everything. Instead, resources are allocated on the basis of where they are likely to be required. When addressing the instruction of frontline staff members, the emphasis in this book is instead focused on devices and their operating systems. Compared with the fluid nature of digital collections, the rate of change on mobile devices is far more manageable.

To address these malleable digital collections, this book advocates relying on vendor help sites or, if they prove insufficient, the creation of staff-maintained help resources.

When changes to these services occur, vendor sites are updated in suit. If you library is maintaining its own resources, they would update them at this time. By leaning on this centralized referral information, you can rapidly adjust to change. Staff members simply continue to apply their device training to a new set of walkthroughs. These resources do not require memorization. Using this model, one or several experienced staff members can quickly correct deficiencies in your staff and patron resources.

In following with a flexible approach to training, the model described allows for staff-directed instruction. With budgets pushed to the breaking point, it is advantageous to libraries to offer relevant training without overly impacting desk coverage. By allowing staff members to train when they can, this impact is eased. Similarly, no staff member is required to train more than is necessary. Aside from the aforementioned levels of training, the ability for a staff member to pass their road test at any time means that staff will not be asked to go through a module if they don't need it. Instead, the focus is on demonstrating the requisite skills to assist your public, whether they were learned at the library or already known.

A COMPREHENSIVE APPROACH TO MARKETING

Acknowledging that many library patrons still are unaware of your digital collection, this book took a comprehensive approach to marketing. With the understanding that patrons access library information in different ways, outlined were methods of reaching your public through mediums both new and traditional. Even using an à la carte approach, you can effectively reach patrons both within and outside the library. In many ways, this book took the familiar and communicated how it could be used to promote this new avenue of library service.

For traditional print marketing, we examined sample copy appropriate for newsletters mailed to your patrons or otherwise used in posters and flyers within your library building. Several methods for getting these flyers into your patron's hands were outlined. We saw how a book or other media display could be modified to promote your digital collection. Methods for tying a virtual collection to your physical one were outlined, from inserts by the library staff to pre-processing options from your distributors.

With the explosion of social media, this book examined several of the most popular sites and offered practical advice on how they could be used to promote your collection. When possible, these methods played to the individual strengths of each. For example, when looking at Pinterest, we took a highly visual approach to showcasing individual titles and collections. In the case of Twitter, our promotions were modified to work within the site's character limit and instead took a headline approach.

Finally, utilizing a device-centered approach, we examined hands-on methods for patrons to learn about and engage your digital collection. From kiosks and gadget petting zoos fixed in place to devices lent to patrons on short- and long-term loan, we saw scalable options you could choose to fit your needs. Some were out of the box, while others, ever cost conscious, were of the do-it-yourself variety.

ENGAGING IN DIGITAL OUTREACH

The nature of digital media allows for it to be borrowed, consumed, and returned without ever entering the library. These natural advantages can often lead a library to ignore valuable outreach opportunities. Acknowledging that not all library patrons enter the library on a regular basis and not all members of your community are cardholders, we applied traditional outreach methods to a library's digital collection. Rather than observe a one-size-fits-all approach, this book outlined numerous approaches that could be undertaken with various-sized staffs and budgets. We started with a small presence, and employing traditional print marketing materials, we worked our way up to an approach that essentially served as a digital branch library! Between those two models were robust service offerings that relied on a few mobile devices, a wireless Internet connection, and a bit of staff ingenuity. Using these methods, you can place library digital media in the hands of patrons who stand to benefit the most from it.

REMOVING BARRIERS TO USE

Ultimately, the best way to conceptualize your challenge is to think of it as removing barriers to use. A gap in awareness exists, with patrons often unaware of the existence and composition of your digital collection. Patrons reaching your library with difficulty or who simply don't do so on a regular basis stand to benefit the most from this digital collection. At the same time, they are often the most difficult to reach. Even when awareness exists, there are still more difficulties.

Your digital collection, more so than your physical one, has numerous requirements, prerequisites, and other hoops to jump through. Not all patrons own devices capable of accessing your collection. Patrons that do may struggle with their basic use, not to mention checking out, downloading, streaming, or otherwise using library digital media. These patrons will need a trained staff ready and willing to assist them at home, in person, or wherever they may be.

Using the approaches outlined in this book, you can work to strip away these barriers to use one by one. A robust approach to marketing builds awareness. Outreach brings your collections, services, and programs to the farthest corners of your community and creates new digital patrons. As these patrons attempt to access your collection, they are able to rely on the help of a well-trained staff. This staff, through a combination of traditional reference, individualized appointments, and group instruction, can build his patron's confidence in the collection and the technology used to consume it. Patrons lacking the required devices have the opportunity to experience the technology through device lending kiosks and gadget petting zoos. It is through this multi-faceted strategy that a library can succeed in making the most of its digital collection.

Appendix

ANTI-THEFT/SECURITY DEVICES AND SOFTWARE

Android Device Manager: Google's device management software, used to locate and remotely wipe a device. https://www.google.com/android/devicemanager

iCloud: In addition to being a cloud storage service, it contains a find feature, allowing you to locate and remotely wipe an iOS device. https://www.icloud.com/

MacLocks: Vendor of enclosures, tethers, and security mounts for a variety of devices. http://www.maclocks.com/

OtterBox: Vendor of heavy-duty phone and mobile device cases. http://www.otterbox.com/

KIOSK HARDWARE AND SOFTWARE

42 Gears Mobility Systems: Software for kiosk mode, mobile device management and lockdown of devices. http://www.42gears.com/

Inteset Secure Lockdown Software: Able to place a Windows computer into kiosk mode.

Overdrive Media Station: Kiosk software showcasing a library's collection of eBooks and eAudiobooks. http://company.overdrive.com/products/overdrive-media-station/

3M Discovery Station: All-in-one eBook station for the 3M Cloud Library, which includes hardware and kiosk software. http://solutions.3m.com/wps/portal/3M/en_US/library-systems-NA/library-technologies/ebook-lending/Cloud-Library-Hardware/

LIBRARY DIGITAL MEDIA SERVICES

Axis 360: Baker & Taylor-owned distributor of eBooks and digital audiobooks to libraries. http://axis360.rightbrainmedia.com/

Comics Plus: Digital comic book service. http://iversecomics.com/library-details/

Flipster: EBSCO-owned digital magazine solution. https://flipster.ebsco.com/

Freading: eBook service that offers immediate access to 50,000 titles, utilizing a pay-per-use model. http://www.libraryideas.com/freading.html

Freegal Movies: A streaming movie service that operates on a subscription model. http://www.libraryideas.com/movies.html

Freegal Music: Streaming and downloadable music and music videos. Music downloads are DRM free and permanent. Files can be transferred to another device capable of playing an MP3, MPEG4. http://www.libraryideas.com/freegal.html

Hoopla: Provider of digital movies, television, music, audiobooks, and other media. http://library.hoopladigital.com/

IndieFlix: Streaming movie service brokered by Recorded Books. Features 6,500 independent films. http://www.recordedbooks.com/index.cfm?fuseaction=rb.indie

OneClickdigital: Provider of eBooks and eAudiobooks to libraries. http://www.oneclickdigital.com/

Overdrive, Inc.: Vendor of eBooks, digital audiobooks, music, and movies. https://www.overdrive.com/

3M Cloud Library: 3M's eBook solution for libraries. http://www.3m.com/us/library/eBook/

Tumblebooks: Offers access to eBooks and eAudiobooks for children and young adults. https://www.tumblebooks.com/

Zinio: Digital magazines. Currently brokered through Recorded Books. http://www.recordedbooks.com/Zinio

Bibliography

Adobe Digital Editions. 2015. "Adobe Digital Editions – FAQs." Accessed January 5, 2015. http://help.axis360.baker-taylor.com/articles/General/Adobe-Digital-Editions-FAQs/.

Amazon. 2015a. "Kindle." Accessed June 1, 2015. https://kindle.amazon.com/.

Amazon. 2015b. "Kindle Fire HD X 7." Accessed June 1, 2015. http://www.amazon.com/dp/B00BWYRF7E/ref=fs_ft.

Amazon Device Support. 2015. "Kindle E-Reader and Fire Tablet User's Guides." Accessed March 1, 2015. http://www.amazon.com/gp/help/customer/display.html?nodeId=200317150.

Android. 2015. "Android Device Manager." Accessed February 12, 2015. https://www.google.com/android/devicemanager.

Android Central. 2015. Accessed April 24, 2015. http://www.androidcentral.com.

Android Official Blog. 2015. Accessed May 7, 2015. http://officialandroid.blogspot.com.

Apple. 2015a. "About Restrictions (Parental Controls) on iPhone, iPad and iPod Touch." Accessed May 29, 2015. https://support.apple.com/en-us/HT201304.

Apple. 2015b. "Hot News." Accessed May 5, 2015. http://www.apple.com/hotnews.

Apple. 2015c. "iCloud: Restore or Setup your iOS Device from iCloud." Accessed May 5, 2015. https://support.apple.com/kb/ph12521?locale=en_US.

Apple. 2015d. "iPad User Guide." Accessed February 12, 2015. http://help.apple.com/ipad/8/.

Apple. 2015e. "Volume Purchase Program for Education." Accessed May 10, 2015. https://volume.itunes.apple.com/store.

Apple Press Info. 2009. "Apple Announces the New iPhone 3GS—The Fastest, Most Powerful iPhone Yet." Accessed May 12, 2015. https://www.apple.com/pr/library/2009/06/08Apple-Announces-the-New-iPhone-3GS-The-Fastest-Most-Powerful-iPhone-Yet.html.

Apple Store. 2015. "Buy Your iPad Mini 3." Accessed June 1, 2015. http://store.apple.com/us/buy-ipad/ipad-mini-3.

ATT. 2015. "Data Calculator." Accessed March 17, 2015. http://www.att.com/att/datacalculator/.

Barnes and Noble. 2015. "NOOK GlowLight." Accessed June 1, 2015. http://www.barnesandnoble.com/p/nook-glowlight-barnes-noble/1114959612?ean=9781400699896.

Blogger. 2015. "Blogger Getting Started Guide." Accessed April 14, 2015. https://support.google.com/blogger/answer/1623800?hl=en&ref_topic=3339243.

BookLending.com. 2015. "FAQ." Accessed May 12, 2015. http://booklending.com/faq.htm.

Brooklyn Public Library. 2015. "Today's Teens, Tomorrow's Techies." Accessed May 5, 2015. http://www.bklynlibrary.org/support/volunteer/t4.

Chattahoochee Valley Libraries. 2015. "Digital Bookmobile." Accessed June 1, 2015. http://www.cvlga.org/digital-bookmobile.

CNET. 2015. "Google Search Has a Newfound Love for Mobile-Friendly Sites." Accessed May 29, 2015. http://www.cnet.com/news/google-search-will-now-favor-mobile-friendly-sites/.

The Computer Language Company. 2015. "PC News Encyclopedia: QR Code." Accessed January 5, 2015. http://www.pcmag.com/encyclopedia/term/61424/qr-code.

ComScore. 2014. "Major Mobile Milestones in May: Apps Now Drive Half of All Time Spent On Digital." Accessed May 15, 2015. http://www.comscore.com/Insights/Blog/Major-Mobile-Milestones-in-May-Apps-Now-Drive-Half-of-All-Time-Spent-on-Digital.

Constant Contact. 2015. Accessed June 1, 2015. http://www.constantcontact.com/.

DigitalBookMobile.com. 2015a. Accessed May 16, 2015. http://digitalbookmobile.com/.

DigitalBookMobile.com. 2015b. "Immerse Yourself in the Digital Bookmobile Experience." Accessed May 16, 2015. http://digitalbookmobile.com/#experience Section.

DigitalBookMobile.com. 2015c. "Contact Us." Accessed May 16, 2015. http://digitalbookmobile.com/#contactSection.

Facebook. 2015. "Advertise on Facebook." Accessed June 1, 2015. https://www.facebook.com/advertising?_rdr.

Factually. 2014. "95 Percent of American Public Libraries Now Carry eBooks." Accessed May 25, 2015. http://factually.gizmodo.com/95-percent-of-american-public-libraries-now-carry-ebook-1663882055#.

Fairport Public Library. 2015a. "Teen Tech Tutor Application." Accessed May 2, 2015. http://www.fairportlibrary.org/component/rsform/form/19-teen-tech-tutor-application.

Fairport Public Library. 2015b. "Teen Volunteers." Accessed May 2, 2015. http://www.fairportlibrary.org/teens/teen-volunteer.

Forbes. 2014. "Do You Borrow eBooks from your Library?" Accessed May 25, 2015. http://www.forbes.com/sites/jeremygreenfield/2014/04/25/do-you-borrow-ebooks-from-your-library/.

42 Gears Mobility Systems. 2015. "Product Documentation." Accessed March 17, 2015. http://www.42gears.com/documentation.html.

Geek. 2010. "Sony Announces First Participants of Reader Library Program." Accessed May 29, 2015. http://www.geek.com/news/sony-announces-first-participants-of-reader-library-program-1287427/.

Google. 2015. "Age Requirements on Google Accounts." Accessed February 12, 2015. https://support.google.com/accounts/answer/1350409?hl=.

Google Chrome. 2015. "Google Chrome Browser." Accessed February 12, 2015. https://www.google.com/chrome/browser/.

Google Docs. 2015. "Google Forms." Accessed February 12, 2015. https://www
.google.com/forms.

Harrison Public Library. 2013. "Social Media Policy." Accessed June 1, 2015. http://
www.harrisonpl.org/social-media-policy.php.

IDC. 2015. "Android and iOS Squeeze the Competition, Swelling to 96.3%
of the Smartphone Operating System Market for Both 4Q14 and CY14,
According to IDC." Accessed March 17, 2015. http://www.idc.com/getdoc
.jsp?containerId=prUS25450615.

Innovative. 2015. "Sierra." Accessed June 1, 2015. http://www.iii.com/products/
sierra.

Kiddoware. 2015. "Kids Place Parental Control." Accessed May 29, 2015. http://
kiddoware.com/app/kids-place-parental-control-for-android-devices/.

LibraryAware. 2015. Accessed June 1, 2015. http://www.libraryaware.com/.

Live-Brary. 2015a. "Free Downloads." Accessed May 29, 2015. http://downloads
.live-brary.com/722A67A0-D179–4A88-A68B-B508ABAC4BA0/10/50/en/
Default.htm.

Live-Brary. 2015b. "SCLS Map." Accessed May 29, 2015. http://www.sclsmap
.info/.

MacRumors. 2015. Accessed May 29, 2015. www.macrumors.com.

Mashable. 2015. "Tech." Accessed May 5, 2015. http://mashable.com/tech/.

Microsoft Office. 2015. "Save as PDF." Accessed April 14, 2015. https://support.office
.com/en-au/article/Save-as-PDF-d85416c5–7d77–4fd6-a216–6f4bf7c7c110.

MMSCL. 2014. "Mastic Moriches Shirley Community Library Mobile App."
Accessed February 1, 2015. http://mmscl.boopsie.com/.

MobileBeacon. 2015. "New York Public Library: Free, At-Home Access and 24/7
Learning Opportunities for NYC Patrons." Accessed May 29, 2015. http://
www.mobilebeacon.org/new-york-public-library/?utm_source=nyplpressre-
lease&utm_medium=email&utm_campaign=nyplpressrelease.

MySA. 2014. "SAPL Launches Digital Literacy Interactive Kiosks for eBook Checkout and Rapid Recharging at the SA International Airport." Accessed May
16, 2015. http://blog.mysanantonio.com/sapl/2014/10/sapl-launches-digital-
library-interactive-kiosks-for-ebook-checkout-and-rapid-recharging-at-the-sa-
international-airport/.

Nexus. 2015. "Nexus Help: Add or Remove an Account." Accessed May 29, 2015.
https://support.google.com/nexus/answer/2840815?hl=en.

9to5Mac. 2014. "iOS and Android Combine to Capture 96% Global Market
Share in Q3." Accessed February 2, 2015. http://9to5mac.com/2014/10/31/
android-vs-ios-market-share-3q-2014/.

Nova Solutions, Inc. 2015. "Square Top Lectern." Accessed June 1, 2015. http://
www.novadesk.com/square-top-lectern.

Office of the US Attorneys. 1854. "Copyright Infringement—First Sale Document." Accessed June 1, 2015. http://www.justice.gov/usam/criminal-resource-
manual-1854-copyright-infringement-first-sale-doctrine.

OSXDaily. 2012. "iOS 6 Compatibility and Supported Devices." Accessed May 5,
2015. http://osxdaily.com/2012/06/13/ios-6-compatibility-supported-devices/.

Otterbox. 2015. Accessed May 29, 2015. http://otterbox.com.

Overdrive. 2014. "Read an eBook Day." Accessed May 29, 2015. http://readanebook
day.com/.

Overdrive. 2015. "eReading Room for Kids or Teens." Accessed March 17, 2015. http://company.overdrive.com/products/ereading-room/.

Overdrive Blogs. 2011. "Broward County Library Makes eBooks Available at Airport." Accessed February 2, 2015. http://blogs.overdrive.com/promotional-ideas/2011/11/28/broward-county-library-makes-ebooks-available-at-airport/.

Overdrive Help. 2015. "Why Aren't There More Copies of a Title Available?" Accessed May 12, 2015. http://help.overdrive.com/customer/portal/articles/1481182-why-aren-t-there-more-copies-of-a-title-available-.

Overdrive Media Station. 2015. "Overdrive Media Station." Accessed February 12, 2015. http://company.overdrive.com/products/overdrive-media-station/.

PC Mag. 2015a. "News." Accessed May 5, 2015. http://www.pcmag.com/news.

PC Mag. 2015b. "What is Cloud Computing?" Accessed May 21, 2015. http://www.pcmag.com/article2/0,2817,2372163,00.asp.

Project Gutenberg. 2015. "Free eBooks by Project Gutenberg." Accessed May 15, 2015. http://www.gutenberg.org/.

Safari. 2009. "How Big Is the Average ePub Book?" Accessed March 17, 2015. https://blog.safaribooksonline.com/2009/11/16/how-big-is-the-average-epub-book/.

Safelite. 2015. "Technician Profile E-mail." Accessed February 2, 2015. https://www.safelite.com/about-safelite/about-safelite/?no_cache=1&sword_list%5B0%5D=photo.

Samsung. 2015a. "Galaxy Tab A." Accessed June 1, 2015. http://www.samsung.com/us/explore/Tab-A-features-and-specs/?cid=ppc-.

Samsung. 2015b. "MicroHDMI to VGA Adapter." Accessed June 1, 2015. http://www.samsung.com/us/computer/pcs-accessories/AA-AH3AUKB/US.

San Jose Mercury News. 2012. "Brentwood Pilot Program Brings eReaders to Homebound." Accessed June 1, 2015. http://www.mercurynews.com/breaking-news/ci_19820094.

Sony Reader Store. 2014. Accessed May 29, 2015. http://ebookstore.sony.com/downpage/index_b.html.

Speed Guide. 2014. "What Is the Actual Real-Life Speed of Wireless Networks." Accessed June 8, 2015. http://www.speedguide.net/faq/what-is-the-actual-real-life-speed-of-wireless-374.

Tech Crunch. 2014. "Amazon Doubles the Storage of the Existing Kindle Paperwhite." Accessed February 5, 2015. http://techcrunch.com/2014/08/15/amazon-doubles-the-storage-of-the-existing-kindle-paperwhite/.

3M. 2015. "3M Discovery Station." Accessed February 12, 2015. http://solutions.3m.com/wps/portal/3M/en_US/library-systems-NA/library-technologies/ebook-lending/Cloud-Library-Hardware/Discovery-Station/.

Time. 2014. "Android Tablets Eat Up a Slice of Apple's Market Share." Accessed February 12, 2015. http://time.com/11384/android-tablets-eat-up-a-slice-of-apples-market-share/.

TopTenReviews. 2015. "2015 Best eBook Reader Reviews and Comparisons." Accessed April 26, 2015. http://ebook-reader-review.toptenreviews.com/.

Twitter. 2015. "Using Twitter with Facebook." Accessed May 29, 2015. https://support.twitter.com/articles/31113-using-twitter-with-facebook.

The Verge. 2013. "iOS: A Visual History." Accessed January 2, 2015. http://www
.theverge.com/2011/12/13/2612736/ios-history-iphone-ipad.

WordPress. 2015. "More Features." Accessed April 14, 2015. https://wordpress
.com/#more-features.

YouTube. 2015. "Create and Delete Playlists." Accessed April 14, 2015. https://
support.google.com/youtube/answer/57792?hl=en.

Index

About the Author

NICHOLAS TANZI is the current Head of Digital Services at the Mastics-Moriches-Shirley Community Library. He earned his master's degree in library science from CUNY Queens College. He has presented extensively on emerging technology in the library, including 3D printing and digital services implementation. When he's not in library land, he can be found reading interactive fiction (playing video games) or walking his dog in downtown Port Jeff with his wife, Kristine.